Contemporary Problems
IN
RELIGION

LEO M. FRANKLIN — 1870-1948

Contemporary Problems

in RELIGION

HAROLD ALBERT BASILIUS, *Editor*

*Holder of the Leo M. Franklin Memorial Chair
in Human Relations at Wayne University
for the year 1953-1954*

Essay Index Reprint Series

BOOKS FOR LIBRARIES PRESS
FREEPORT, NEW YORK

111861

STANDARD BOOK NUMBER:
8369-1545-3

LIBRARY OF CONGRESS CATALOG CARD NUMBER:
78-93315

PRINTED IN THE UNITED STATES OF AMERICA

*The Leo M. Franklin Lectures in Human Relations
and Occupants of the Leo M. Franklin Memorial
Chair in Human Relations at Wayne University*

1950–51 TOWARD BETTER HUMAN RELATIONS
LLOYD ALLEN COOK
Professor of Educational Sociology

1951–52 OUR TROUBLES WITH DEFIANT YOUTH
FRITZ REDL
Professor of Social Work

1952–53 AMERICAN FOREIGN POLICY AND
AMERICAN DIPLOMACY
ALFRED H. KELLY
Professor of History

1953–54 THE ROLE OF RELIGION IN HUMAN
RELATIONS
HAROLD A. BASILIUS
Professor of German

1954–55 DEMOCRATIC VALUES AND PROBLEMS OF
POWER IN AMERICAN SOCIETY
ARTHUR KORNHAUSER
Professor of Psychology

Preface

THE LECTURES in this volume, embracing the fourth
in the series of Leo M. Franklin Memorial Lectures in
Human Relations heard annually at Wayne University,
were given during the academic year 1953-54.

Temple Beth El of Detroit, which the late Dr. Leo M.
Franklin served as rabbi from 1899 to 1941 and as rabbi
emeritus till his death in 1948, established a chair at Wayne
University in 1950 to commemorate the person and work
of its great and beloved spiritual leader. Because his
ministry was especially distinguished by its concern for
the improvement of human relations in all areas of living,
the chair established to honor his memory was appropri-
ately designated the Leo M. Franklin Memorial Chair in
Human Relations. Each year a committee of the faculty
recommends to the President of Wayne University some
member of the faculty who shall be the occupant of the
Memorial Chair and thus also the Leo M. Franklin
Memorial Professor for that year. It is the obligation of
the Franklin Memorial Professor to organize and present
a series of lectures dealing with some important phase of
human relations in contemporary American life.

The focus of the present volume of lectures, which have
been printed with only minor variations from the form
in which they were heard, is an attempted reassessment
of the problem and role of religion in contemporary life.
All of the lectures assume that religious experience is a

basic dimension of living and each, therefore, addresses itself to one or several problems, theoretical or practical, which result from this assumption, particularly in a society such as ours, which is so conscious and even proud of its rational, empirical, and "practical," that is to say, its areligious, orientation. That Rabbi Leo M. Franklin made his fine contributions to the improvement of human relations chiefly as a minister to the religious needs of his fellow men perhaps lends to these particular lectures an additional appropriateness.

To Temple Beth El, to Mr. Leo I. Franklin and his family, and to my colleagues in Wayne University I should like here formally to record my genuine and great gratitude for the honor and privilege of occupying the Franklin Chair during the past year. To the following colleagues and friends I owe special thanks for counsel and assistance in organizing the series: William Bossenbrook, Milton Covensky, Max Kapustin, Orville Linck, James Maguire, Robert Moore, Victor Rapport, Margaret Sterne, Chalmers Wickwire.

HAROLD A. BASILIUS

Detroit, January 1955

Contents

AUSLÄNDER

Engelmillionen
Fahrend weg und zu
Die im Himmel wohnen
Treffen Heimat nie dazu.

CHESTER F. KUHN
12 May 1954

INTRODUCTION: Why Religion in the American University?

As A POET and an artist I am a polytheist; but as a natural scientist, a pantheist; and the one I am as decisively as the other. When I need a God for myself personally, as an ethical being, this, too, is provided for. The celestial and terrestrial matters are so wide a realm, that only the organs of all beings together are able to comprehend it.

—Goethe in a letter to Jakobi.

Introduction

SINCE THE Franklin Memorial Chair is one in human relations and since each incumbent of the Chair has the exclusive determination of the topic for the annual lectures during his tenure, a word of explanation is in order regarding the choice of topic for this year and its connection with the vast area of human relations.

The following three reasons underlie my choice of the topic of the role of religion in human affairs:

In the first place, with most of my colleagues I regard a university as being primarily a community of scholars who have the twofold function of continuously investigating any and all problems, including the problems of culture, and of trying continuously by all available means to transmit the residue of their investigations to their students.

It follows that a university is the one place created deliberately and intentionally for that purpose by society where so-called controversial questions may be investigated and discussed publicly without the implication that the discussant is either categorically pro or con whatever he happens to be discussing.

Since all questions in this sense of the term "question" are "controversial," the phrase is redundant. Our propensity for emphasizing this redundancy is a sign of the sickness of our time. The sickness results from the suppression and repression of free thought and free speech. The redundant term "controversial question" suggests that there are two kinds of questions, namely those which may and those which may not be publicly discussed. I am suggesting that the idea of a university represents precisely the reverse of such a notion.[1]

In spite of the fact that religion has been and is one of the great motivating forces in human relations, it tends also, unfortunately, to come under the heading of controversial questions. So does Communism, for that matter, and, incidentally, the religious aspect of Communism is worth noting in this connection. That religion is controversial is true, at least, in our country and in my profession. In proposing to discuss the question of religion publicly, I propose, therefore, also to be severely critical of American culture and of my profession. I say this not in the way of a preliminary apology. I say it simply to emphasize the notion that a university is an institution dedicated to precisely this kind of criticism. It goes without saying, of course, that the criticism should be constructive and in the spirit of "whom the Lord loveth he chasteneth." I might add that I think that mentioning the necessity for continuous constructive criticism is all the more important in a time such as ours which stresses with almost pathological insistence the desirability and even necessity for everyone to get along, as the saying goes, with everyone else. But when the pressures to universal conformity become so great as to stifle healthy disagreement, a university, particularly one in a democratic society, would be remiss in its social obligations if it did not resist these pressures by deliberately provoking public discussion of so-called controversial questions.

In thus defining a university I should, however, like to make very explicit that I have not even a remote conception of the university as an ivory tower. I make no

4

bones about the fact that from my point of view all learning, if it be valid, must be useful.

The problem of religion has suffered neglect, however, not only because it is controversial. The press of day-to-day problems in a world so complex as ours, the cry for the immediate, pragmatic solution of these problems, the enormity of our scholarship and knowledge which can be applied to the solution of these great problems, these readily make for a situation in which basically important theoretical problems are neglected. I continue to be interested in trying to understand more thoroughly the reasons underlying the neglect of religious problems.

There is a well established consensus regarding the gradual secularization of our culture since roughly the fourteenth century. And the term " secularization " already implies the lesser importance of religion in the culture. I doubt that we need to discuss this observation any further.

It is my feeling, however, that there are components of American culture, biases or prejudices of the culture, if you will, which have contributed to an even more basic neglect of the problem of religion than is the case in other subcultures of the Western cultural complex. Perhaps they have to do with what Mr. George K. Kennan, our former ambassador to Russia, referred to in his convocation address last May at the University of Notre Dame as " a deep-seated weakness in the American character; a certain shy self-consciousness that tends to deny interests other than those of business, sport, or war. There is a powerful strain of our American cast of mind that has little use for the artist or the writer." [2]

The exaggerated biases of American culture are in my opinion twofold. One is the bias of excessive rationalism

5

or, as one of my colleagues recently referred to it, the empirical-rational tradition of Anglo-American culture. With reference to the problem of religion, this means an inclination to refer all questions of religion to ecclesiastical or political organization of one sort or another. It means an impatience with and even a contempt for discussion of basic theoretical problems such as the existence or non-existence of God, or the ultimate source and criteria of values in so far as these relate to religious assumptions. Such matters are disposed of as being " mentalistic " or " medieval," or " metaphysical " or " mystical," in any case impractical and therefore worthless analogues in the last instance to the proverbial scholastic propensity for wasting time in discussing such questions as how many angels can dance on the point of a pin. The important things are, by contrast, business, sport, or war, as Mr. Kennan suggests.

There has been considerable recent comment on the excessive rationalist bias of our culture. Reinhold Niebuhr, for example, after characterizing Gilbert Highet's highly regarded recent book *Man's Unconquerable Mind* as being " a lyrical account of the triumphs of culture and the relation of man's intellectual faculties to those triumphs," goes on to say: " We must no doubt resist every effort to restrain the human mind and bend every effort to enlarge the scope of its knowledge. But human history is more complex and more tragic than is suggested in this excellent panegyric on the glories of the intellect of man." [3]

Bound up with the rationalist bias of American culture is its optimism, regarding which H. B. Parkes, in a review of Ralph Barton Perry's *Realms of Value*, writes as follows: " As with American society in general, one is left some-

what torn between admiration for the qualities of gener-
osity and good will which it displays and fear lest its
optimism about human nature may prevent a realistic
approach to the crises of twentieth century civilization." [4]

The classical remark apropos of this whole point is
probably one that Alexis de Tocqueville made in his
Democracy in America in a chapter headed " Why the
Americans are more addicted to practical than to theoretical science " (Vol. II, First Book, Chapter X). The
remark reads: " Those who cultivate the sciences amongst
a democratic people are always afraid of losing their way
in visionary speculation. They mistrust systems; they
adhere closely to facts and the study of facts with their
own senses."

The other bias of our culture is actually corollary to
the first and has particular relevance to the neglect of
religious problems. I refer to the concomitants of our
long established tradition of the separation of church and
state. It is our traditional inclination to feel that questions
of religion belong exclusively in the church, and by implication not in the schools, including, of course, the university. It has always seemed to me remarkably strange
that a people such as ours which boasts of its independence
and self-reliance could build such a bogey-man out of
religion with the result, and I think it is socially an expen-
sive one, that the universities have been sterilized for
a hundred years or more of the investigation or discussion
of basic religious, not to mention theological, problems.
In saying this, I should perhaps mention that I am not
following the line here of young Mr. William Buckley's
God and Man at Yale. His interest was propagandizing a
reactionary position. Mine is simply to point up a fact
of our cultural history.

I am reminded here of the observation of Friedrich Nietzsche regarding the reintroduction of Eastern thought into the West at the hands of Arthur Schopenhauer early in the nineteenth century. The last great cultural import from the East, which came just prior to the decline of the Roman Empire, was the Christian idea of other-worldliness and the ethic of selflessness, until Schopenhauer in the early nineteenth century re-interpreted the wisdom of the Vedas. In so doing, however, Schopenhauer also unwittingly revitalized the sacred tradition of Christianity in its Asiatic aspects. That he did so caused Nietzsche to exclaim with exultation: " We have turned reaction into progress! " (See " Progress and Reaction " in *Menschliches Allzumenschliches*) .[5] This incident moved Thomas Mann to a discourse on what he happily, in my opinion, called the modern rationalism of the irrational. By this term he put his finger on a point of great importance. Whereas the rationalist bias of our culture has tended to mark everything called irrational as substandard and suspect, modern psychological and psychoanalytic researches have taught us the importance and even indispensability of religious faith and the cultural significance of myths, including the great religious myths. In short, these researches have given a renewed scientific emphasis to the importance for individual and social health of the irrational in our lives. Freud's application of the image of the iceberg, eight-ninths of which is submerged while only the one-ninth is visible, to the proportion of the irrational and rational components of our personalities graphically illustrates the power and importance of better comprehending and evaluating the irrational. Thus Mann's implied distinction between the rejection, on the one hand, of the old and naïvely over-simple dichotomy of rational vs. irrational, and the acceptance on the other hand of the new and modern notion of a rationalism of the irrational is very pertinent to the kind of renewed emphasis which our time needs and apparently wants to give to religious phenomena. "Current events," says Franz Alexander, "impress us with their irrationality. . . . The dominance of irrational forces in human nature has perhaps never been as complete as at the present moment." [6]

My third and final reason for choosing the role of religion in human affairs as the topic for the lecture series of this year is my observation in the last half dozen years of the intense interest of my students and of students in general in information and direction with reference to religion and its role in their own individual lives. Some of my colleagues will disagree with me about the validity of this observation, but I would cite a corroborating and revealing statistic in this connection. Mr. Eugene Exman recently reported that the figures for book sales for the year 1949 showed that four out of five best selling non-fiction items bore religious titles. He follows this observation by quoting Professor Halford E. Luccock of Yale, who wrote in *Publisher's Weekly* that in the current interest in religious books we are witnessing "one of the most striking changes in feeling, mood, and taste which have occurred in centuries, [taking place] not as changes in literary trends have usually occurred, over a generation or half a century, but telescoped into a very few years." [7]

Perhaps the current interest of students in religion is aptly characterized by Erich Fromm's remark that "most people ' believe ' in monotheism, while their actual devotion belongs to systems which are, indeed, much closer to totemism and the worship of idols than any form of

Christianity." [8] I incline to believe that many students are vaguely aware of this kind of ambiguity and confusion in their own make-up and properly look to the university for clarification of it.

In thus delineating my reasons for devoting this year's lectures to the role of religion in human affairs, I should add that I personally am not a religious man in the sense that I am an adherent or a promoter of organized religion. I do, however, have an intense interest in religion both as a human being and as a scholar and teacher. In both capacities I am continuously impressed with the enormous motivating force of religion in human thought and action both in the past and in the present and the utter legitimacy of religion as something all-too-human in that tragic but loving sense of Nietzsche's phrase. As a professional teacher of the humanities, I could not avoid questions of religious values, even if I wanted to, for, after all, the proper study of mankind is man, as Stuart Chase again has recently reminded us in the title of one of his books. Beyond that, however, I believe with Goethe that " religion is not an end but a means of attaining the highest human development through the purest tranquility of spirit."

One of the celebrated causes of our day, McCarthyism, neatly illustrates the confusion that results from the over-emphasis of the rationalist-intellectualist strain in our culture and the under-emphasis of the religious. McCarthyism is frequently explained as an aspect, perhaps the most pertinent one, of what is referred to as the wave of anti-intellectualism which has been sweeping our country. Aside from not knowing precisely what anti-intellectualism means in this context, I think the observation is basically fallacious. McCarthy presents a simple problem in public morality which is the identical problem posed by Hitler and imperialist Communism twenty years ago. The problem is simply whether or not traditional principles of right and wrong, of truth and falsehood, of the sanctity of the individual and of human dignity generally still obtain or whether we are ready to return to jungle ethics. It is this threatening trans-valuation of all of the inherited and traditional values that causes uneasiness rather than any notion of the relationship of McCarthy to intellectualty or anti-intellectuality of any kind.[9]

H. A. B.

CHAPTER ONE

Faith and the Dilemma
of the
Educated Man

FRED BERTHOLD, JR.

Chairman, Department of Religion
Dartmouth College

Faith and the Dilemma
of the Educated Man

SOME TIME AGO I ran across a cartoon which showed a man, obviously a long-haired intellectual, standing in a fashionable art gallery, looking at a picture. The cartoonist had succeeded in suggesting a genuine pathos in the features of this man, who was saying to himself, " I know everything about Art, but I don't know what I like." This may illustrate what I mean by the dilemma of the modern, educated man. It has been his characteristic passion to " know everything." It has been his characteristic lot to feel increasingly bewildered as to what he ought to " like." Chock full of more and more information, he has felt less and less capable of deciding what is good and what is bad. Master of how things work, he has come to feel futile before the question about the end for which they ought to work.

This dilemma might be due to several things. It might be due to the fact that our approach to problems of value is not right. Or it might be due to the fact that the more we know about the world, the more we realize that there really are no objective values. This latter point of view has been powerfully and succinctly expressed by Joseph Wood Krutch in his widely read book, *The Modern Temper*. Mr. Krutch would describe the dilemma very much as we have done, but he would account for it differently. While man still very much desires to believe that there is purpose and a standard of the good in life, the progress of science increasingly reveals that we live in a world in which values have no objective status. Man needs ethical standards by which to live, and he instinctively seeks them. His intellect, however, is making it clear to him that this is an infantile wish, that nature does not heed and makes no place for his conceptions of good and evil. As Krutch puts it, man is ". . . an ethical animal in a universe which contains no ethical element." This results in a division within man himself. "Try as he may, the two halves of his soul can hardly be made to coalesce, and he cannot either feel as his intelligence tells him that he should feel or think as his emotions would have him think, and thus he is reduced to mocking his torn and divided soul." [1] There is no place for values in this world of fact, except within the shadowy illusions of mankind; and these illusions are being dispelled by the advance of scientific knowledge.

Krutch would agree that, although the illusion is being dispelled, the yearning remains. For we can hardly live together as a community, nor can we find purpose as individuals, if we do not believe that there is something which is worthy of the devotion of every man in every age and every class or nation. Without such a belief, Krutch admits, we "lapse into anarchy." Many of us, after the experiences of the second world conflict, would be tempted to say that the words, "lapse into anarchy," are too tame to express what happens when the belief in objective and universal ethical standards loses its effective hold upon men. And yet many of us ask ourselves: However tragic it may be, is not a man like Krutch right? Is it not increasingly difficult to maintain that the belief in objective values may be intellectually respectable? Is not the idea of the good the result of wishful thinking?

16

It is not accidental that the philosophical movements most characteristic of our time reflect just this radical question. That philosophy which has been called "logical positivism" has had a very far-reaching influence in our day. When asked if he could briefly summarize this philosophy, one wit had the following to say: "The important is unknowable, and the knowable is unimportant." It has always seemed to me that this description contains a considerable measure of justice. Yet it is difficult altogether to escape being drawn into the positivistic mood. Any escape from it in our day is apt to be accomplished by embracing that other fashionable philosophy, existentialism. With regard to our topic, however, the fires of this hell burn very much like those of the former. For the existentialist, too, assures us that there is no way for finite man to discover a norm of the good which transcends himself.

So it is that the educated man in our day has felt at home in the pursuit of objective facts, but ill at ease before the question of good and evil. To get an education has meant, by and large, to seek to rip away the veil of mystery from one area after another until one gets to some objective, bedrock set of facts upon which all men can agree. The most damning phrase which can be spoken by the educated man is, "That's just *your* opinion." Allegiance to a set of values has a taint of unrespectability unless those values can be proven to the impartial judge; and the educated man is increasingly beset by doubts that this can be done.

I remember a conversation I had with a research scientist friend of mine shortly after the A-bomb was dropped on Hiroshima. A number of atomic physicists had become quite excited over the moral issues involved. There were arguments and counterarguments in the *Bulletin of the*

17

Atomic Scientists.[2] In one issue of this journal a promi-
nent scientist raised the question as to whether he and his
colleagues ought not to refuse to do any further work
on atomic fission, since it could evidently be put to such
horrible uses. My friend said something like the following:
" It's awfully presumptuous of that fellow to set his moral
judgment over against that of the vast majority of his
community." And a moment later he added, " If it were
a question of scientific fact, he would have to report his
findings no matter how unpopular they might be. But in
the case of a moral opinion, one has nothing solid to go
on. It's all a subjective thing."

Those who seek to work with problems of value are
often hounded by a feeling of inferiority. In this area
why can't we produce results as the scientists do? *Their*
arguments often lead to new advances of knowledge. *Ours*
go on endlessly and produce only rancour and suspicion.
So ill at ease are those whose interest and training still
call them to work in the realm of values that they are
often tempted to ape the techniques of the quantitative
sciences. One example of this was reported some time ago
in the pages of *The New Yorker*.[3] The editor reported
receiving in the mail a gadget called a " Reading-ease
Calculator." The genius of the device was that you could
apply it to any given bit of written material and thereby
discover its quality. All subjective evaluation was eliminated. Presumably the need for all highly paid literary
editors was also eliminated, a fact which gave some concern
to the gentleman who reported this in *The New Yorker*.
All you had to do to operate this calculator was to set a
little dial according to certain instructions, twirl an indi-
cator in a certain way, and read the verdict which was
delivered in one of four categories: very hard, hard, easy,

and very easy. The booklet of instructions informed one that this also constituted a rating of the excellence of the material: the easier the better. Our editor reports that his first application of the device was to the booklet of instructions which accompanied it. This rated "very hard," and, in this case at least, he was inclined to respect the little gadget.

The dilemma which we face, and the explanation of it which is given by men like Krutch, cannot be understood apart from its historical context. It is directly related to the way in which the ideal of scientific knowledge has been transmitted to our day. Certainly the generative idea of our historical epoch has been science. The modern era was born when men began to turn their attention away from the problem of life beyond the grave to that of the understanding and the conquest of nature. Though the new spirit was abroad before his time, René Descartes gives it classic expression.

> It is possible to attain knowledge which is very useful in life, and . . . instead of that speculative philosophy which is taught in the Schools, we may find a practical philosophy by means of which, knowing the force and the action of fire, water, air, the stars, heavens and all other bodies that environ us, . . . we can in the same way employ them in all those uses to which they are adapted, and thus render ourselves the masters and possessors of nature.[4]

There are no doubt many scientists who may be interested, not in possessing nature, but in understanding her. However it may be with them, there can be little doubt that our civilization has valued science chiefly for its practical gifts.

19

But the utility of science was found to be related to the precise, quantitative methods which she adopted in place of the medieval quest for purposes or final causes. It was necessary to conceive nature as a system of fixed and precise laws which could be mathematically described before man could make much progress in mastering her. The question became not "why" but "how" nature operates. The more precise man's knowledge of "how" became, the more he was able to turn the mechanisms of nature to his own uses. But this also implied that nature herself had no purposes of her own. Galileo put it this way:

> Nature is inexorable and immutable, and never passes the bounds of the laws assigned her, as one that nothing careth, whether her abstruse reasons and methods of operating be or be not exposed to the capacity of men.[5]

Values, purposes are banished from nature's objective order. And modern man has been puzzled ever since as to where, if anywhere, they may reside.

So successful was science in mastering nature, that it was not long before man dreamed of mastering himself and his society. Why could not a Galileo or a Newton arise who would establish an objective science of man and society? Man's reason had laid bare the inner secrets of nature, had traced truth to her source. It only remained to apply the proper methods to these new areas. Prophets of a positive science of society arose. Comte, for example, proclaimed the dawn of the Religion of Humanity. Once the immutable laws which govern the actions of men, both individually and in groups, are formulated, it should be possible to plan for the improvement of society. Indeed, the hope was so intense that many would hear no talk

20

of any limits to the possible progress of man. The belief that reason would provide guidance for the improvement of society influenced men to rebel or to ignore what they regarded as the outmoded authorities of the past.

Modern man, cut loose from traditional authorities, has not, however, realized the fruition of his hope for a positive science of society, for the rational guidance of the community of man to the good life. It is impossible here to describe all of the factors which have eaten into this rationalistic faith and have replaced it with a basket of skepticism, if not cynicism. We may note that there was something strange about this faith in the progress of society through science from the very beginning. It regarded the natural sciences as its model and inspiration. But the prophets of a positive, scientific Religion of Humanity were not sufficiently curious about the paradox of trying to " improve " society with the tools of that science which had proclaimed itself free from questions of value. Curiosity at this point might have led them to suspect either that science was not really entirely independent of questions of value or that their own enterprise was impossible. They accepted the gifts of science uncritically. We might say, if you will pardon a bad metaphor, that they provided their gift horse with a set of false teeth and then refused to look him in the mouth. In these latter days, however, the scientists themselves, under the banner of positivism or operationalism, are telling us that it was all a mistake ever to suppose that science could tell us anything either about ultimate reality or about the good.

We are the heirs of this history. We have been thoroughly imbued with respect for reason and science. We feel that we must have knowledge which is the fruit of evident facts and logical theory before we can commit ourselves. Yet the need for commitment presses upon us even while we seek in vain for a conclusive verdict from our accumulated knowledge. I have had students study religion with me who, at the end of a descriptive, historical course, have been disappointed or even a little angry because the course did not give them a faith. Some of them have seemed to feel that if I had only assigned the right book, or somehow exposed them to just the right combination of facts, the question of this faith or that faith or no faith would have resolved itself. Curiously enough, the same men often complain that faith is purely subjective and relative. This self-contradiction is a symptom of the dilemma which is found almost everywhere in those educational endeavors which are concerned with human values.

We could dwell at length upon the repercussions of this dilemma. I should like briefly to refer to two. It seems to me that what has been called the "depersonalization" of man is directly related to this dilemma. Those centers of meaning and purpose which once were provided for the individual by traditional authorities and by widely shared religious and moral beliefs have been weakened by the modern critique of everything not based upon evident rational principles. The individual has been thrown more upon his own resources and upon his primary relationships for a sense of the meaning and purpose of his own existence. But at the same time his relationships have become more and more impersonal. Technological advances created vast economic systems and crowded, impersonal, urban living conditions. Greater portions of the individual's time and effort went into meeting the demands of a system of which he was but a tiny, and usually a personally insignificant, part. No longer vitally related to religious and moral values which transcend his immediate situation, modern man has been tempted to define himself as a person more and more in terms of the function which he performs in the system. He has come to be known not by who he is but by what he does. From the point of view of the system, however, the function might just as well be performed by another, by any other with the requisite skill.

A very powerful symbol of this depersonalization can be found in Arthur Miller's play, *Death of a Salesman*. Willie, the salesman, allows himself to be defined as a person largely by his function in the economic system. When he can no longer fulfill that function, he can no longer understand himself. His firm doesn't want him any more. He protests, "You can't eat the orange and throw the peel away—a man is not a piece of fruit!" But he doesn't really believe his own protest. He feels that he is nothing, that his only further function in life is to see that his family gets his life insurance. The whole thing is summed up by his son, who says over Willie's grave, "The man didn't know who he was." [6]

Another repercussion of the dilemma of modern man is what I shall call "the tyranny of the present moment." When one believes that the quest for the good is meaningful, he may involve himself in the task which is the essence of all good, liberal education: namely, to allow himself to be confronted by the best that has been thought and believed by men in all ages. He may seek to measure and criticize his own vision of the good against those values which have provided the generative drive for other cultures and other times. On the other hand, if one ever comes to feel that all values are merely a reflection of a subjective bias, then he cannot take any of them seriously, either his own or those of others. Instead of perspective in history, he sees only the drama of the will to power. If values are rooted not in the nature of things but only in personal desires, there is no reason why individuals or nations should not do everything possible to make their own desires prevail. Furthermore, there is no vantage point from which one might be critical of whatever values happen to prevail in one's own society. Whenever people simply accept *what is* because the concept of *what ought to be* has lost all meaning, they have no resources with which to meet or resist naked power. The crazy gyrations of recent world history, the ups and downs of totalitarian movements, are directly related to the lack of securely rooted value commitments in the life of modern man. Having lost his relation to a good which transcends his immediate situation, he has become subject to the tyranny of the present moment.

You may say to me, suppose that we accept, at least in general, your description of the dilemma of the modern, educated man: How can there be any solution to it? I must say that personally I see no hope for a solution if we accept the explanation of the dilemma which men like Mr. Krutch offer. But at the very outset we suggested another possibility: namely, that the dilemma is due to a mistaken approach to the problem of value. I should like to suggest why I think this is the case and how a different approach may once again give meaning to our quest for the good. First of all, however, I should like to record my conviction that the solution which I wish to suggest is not a solution in the sense of removing all our problems. This is, of course, what some people want: not only to have a sense that the quest for the good is humanly significant, but, so to speak, to possess the good as a kind of wand with which to make all problems disappear. The solution to our dilemma does not allow us to escape the tragic elements of all human living, the irrational surd against which men in every age have struggled and agonized. It is a solution in the sense of introducing perspective into the struggle, of giving human meaning to the tragedy. It does not remove us from the whirlwind; but it is a gentle voice in the midst of the whirlwind.

The dilemma of modern man, the gulf between fact and value, may be seen to be a false dilemma when we realize what modern man has sought to forget: that there is no such thing as a significant fact apart from some value context. There is for man no value-free Archimedean point from which he may survey a realm of pure, objective fact. The Cartesian dualism between a world of pure mathematical extension on the one hand, and a world of spiritual purposes and evaluations on the other, is a sophisticated, abstract theory which does not correspond with the actual experience of any man. For real, living human beings (in contrast to hypothetical pure reason) there is no possibility of apprehending the significance of a single fact out of relation to the evaluative perspective which we embody in every moment of our lives.

This does not mean that there are no facts. There are facts which may transcend any given value perspective. Hindus, Christians, and Communists can agree on the laws of the pressure of gases. For special purposes, men may agree to speak about and concern themselves with a system of objective relations which is expressed in an empirical law. But as men they cannot isolate the significance of the law from the perspective with which they evaluate their world as a whole. The bare fact may be recognized. But in addition men are always engaged in interpreting the

25

significance of facts, seeing them in relation to their interpretation of life as a whole. To be sure, if we are honest
and not overly compulsive, new facts may modify or even
seriously challenge the interpretative and evaluative perspective which we bring to them. But what I am trying
to say is that we do not begin in our quest for truth with
a string of bare facts and only later begin to interpret
and evaluate them. As soon as we begin to discern meanings at all, we do so in terms of an evaluative framework
which is a part of our deepest self. The *tabula rasa* of
John Locke is nowhere to be found.[7]

I have spoken clumsily of an " evaluative perspective."
This general phrase may refer to either of two things. If
our evaluative perspective is absorbed uncritically, even
unconsciously, from our parents and social group, I should
prefer to speak of it as " prejudice." For it then becomes
an instrument for pre-judging issues without full awareness of the alternatives. One whose evaluative perspective
is of this kind is like the philosopher of whom it was said,
" He regards as axiomatic every notion which he learned
before he was five years of age." If, however, our evaluative perspective is an expression of our active, critical,
self-conscious awareness, I should prefer to call it " faith."
This may seem to some a strange use of the word " faith."
For many have come to think of it in the manner of that
Sunday School boy who, when asked for a definition, said,
" Faith is believing what you know ain't so." But I am
convinced that my usage conforms to the fundamental
phenomenon to which this word has been applied in the
lives of faithful men. Faith is the active involvement of
the total self in what one regards as worthy of devotion.
As an expression of the total self, it must include the
faithfulness of man's critical faculties. Faith includes more

than our best thinking, but it does include that. Genuine faith does not exclude but embraces even the most radical questioning of man. I have argued that every man actually does interpret facts according to some evaluative perspective. It is unrealistic to assume that this situation will be overcome. We should rather hope that men may come to see the significance of their facts in the light of faith rather than in the murk of prejudice.

I drop two objects. I record the fact that they strike the floor at the same time. If there be among us any Hindus, Moslems, Communists whose faculties are normal and who are honest in their reports, I would expect agreement concerning this fact from all of them. But so far as I am concerned with the bare fact, it is trivial. It takes on no genuinely human significance until it is incorporated into a broader vision of the world. I look at the two objects again. One is large, heavy, inert, inelastic. The other is small, light, elastic. How is it that they fall at the same speed even though they are so different? As soon as I say that this fact has significance for all of nature, that very diverse things in nature may be described mathematically according to the same quantitative laws, then I have entered into a new and revolutionary world-view. The human significance which gives this fact its context is further broadened and deepened, if I should add: the quest for this kind of mathematical law is a highly important thing for man to engage in. Here we have an instance of a fact being clothed by faith. The fact is taken up into a perspective within which alone it achieves significance for man. In essence, I have just described the revolution of Galileo and Descartes.

If we could ever have facts by themselves, apart from a context of value, they would be inert. They would even be fundamentally inert if the context of value were prejudice rather than faith. The creative element in human life is faith. The secret of the creative power of faith lies in the fact that it mobilizes the self to move forward on two fronts—the intellectual and the moral. On the intellectual front, faith is the positive willingness to venture to propose new conceptions, new hypotheses which go beyond what can be demonstrated at the moment. Galileo believed in the possibility of describing the most various natural phenomena by means of simple, mathematical laws. He could not *know* this until he acted in faith, until he worked and thought and disciplined his time and faculties in the belief that he was right. But faith is also creative in the realm of values. It not only acts upon our conception of *what is* but it creatively affirms *what ought to be*. More than this, faith asserts that there is an unbreakable link between the two, that what ought to be is supported by what is. Faith is not belief merely; it is devotion. If we try to begin with a collection of " bare facts " and if we expect these somehow to issue in a vision of the good, we shall be disappointed. But faith begins with a vision of the good and devotion to it, and it seeks to transform the world in obedience to its vision. This does not mean that faith seeks to flout fact, for it includes the faithfulness of the mind and must, therefore, be consistent with our best attested facts.

Modern man has sought to act as if he were a pure mind beholding pure facts. To the extent that he has convinced himself that this is his proper nature and proper business, he has been frustrated in his life as a valuing being and has failed to find a steadying sense of the purpose and significance of his existence. But man is not pure reason. He is a total personality for whom faithful commitment is the expression of the deepest and most natural basis for living. Reason is meant to be a part of the life of faith. Modern man has been misled by the fact that reason is a profoundly important part of the life of faith into believing that it is the whole. But when one seeks to detach reason from its total context, the organism of human life sickens.

This, then, is the general consideration which I should like to bring forth: that man must live by a faith which gives significance and purpose to his collection of facts. Before leaving this general point, I should like to suggest two additional reasons for my belief that faith is necessary in the life of man.

In the first place, as men we are creatures in time. We might almost better say that time is in us. We are not eternal. There was a time when we were not, and there will again be a time when we are not, so far at least as our finite, human nature is concerned. Furthermore, our particular place in history makes a great difference to us. Real time for us is filled with centers of meaning and especially with moments of decision. The things which most concern us comfort us in a particular moment, and our relation to them is decisively determined by how we act then. Whereas the ideal of science is to make time irrelevant, so that the experiment or observation may be repeated by anyone at any time, the things which concern us most as human beings are relevant to time. We must often decide *now*, in this unique time and novel situation. And we must often decide before all of the possible relevant data is in or before it may be subsumed under some category of our knowledge. We must live by faith because we must act in the present moment. When the moment is past and the opportunity for detached reflection arises, the decision has already been made, one way or the other. It is easy to say in retrospect that the United States was right to extend lend-lease aid to Britain in the early days of the recent war. But in the moment of decision there seemed to be no clear light, no certain solution to the problem. We had to act, and we did—in faith.

There is a famous analogy to this reason for the need for faith in William James' essay, " The Will to Believe." [8] He pictures a man standing on a mountain pass. Suddenly a blizzard comes, and he is caught there. It seems that if he tries to stay on the pass, he will surely freeze. Yet he knows that the path down the mountain is tricky. He did not take his bearings carefully enough as he came up, and he is very doubtful if he can find the way. What is he going to do? Shall he refuse to move because he does not know the path, because it is probable, indeed, that he shall go astray? This surely is not reasonable, for he feels that he will freeze unless he does act. In theory, one ought not to act until one knows the answer. But in actuality, this man in this situation faces a forced and momentous choice. To refuse to act is itself an act. Not to decide is a momentous decision.

There is another and closely related reason why we as men must live by faith. The most important things in life can be known only *after* we participate in them or involve ourselves with them. Faith must precede knowledge wherever we are dealing not with abstract relations between objects but with living realities. Though this is true of our relation to such things as political or religious communities, I think that the point can be made clearest in terms of our relations to other persons. Think, in prospect or in retrospect, of that fateful moment in which you are trying to come to a decision: shall I or shall I not propose to this woman (or accept the proposal of this man)? No matter how zealous you may have been in collecting information about this person or in trying to appreciate what this person is really like, many questions remain unanswered. One cannot finally determine if the other will make a good spouse, except by marrying. To be sure, one can estimate probabilities, and one is a fool not to do so. But many of the qualities of the other person you would like to know about are qualities which will be revealed to you only after the relationship of trust and acceptance has been established. One must accept the other in faith or trust before one comes to know the other at a level profound enough to warrant a judgment.

In the realm of religion, too, we can know only as we participate. This is true because God is not an " object." His relation to man is personal in quality. He is not a set of propositions to be assented to, but a Life to be lived with. He can be known only as we involve ourselves with Him in trust, and celebrate His presence in our lives. What I am arguing against, whether it be in life generally or in religion, is a kind of " spectator attitude." Modern man has been beset by the spectator attitude, the attitude of sitting on the sidelines and observing life before entering into it. Is this not a kind of death-urge, this ideal of arresting the movement of life by objectifying it before one dares to enter it? In every important area of life, participation in a community of the faithful is a prerequisite to a full understanding of the meaning of faith.

In closing, I should like to say just a word about a more special consideration which I believe may help to provide perspective upon the dilemma of modern man. It is related to the question which, I am sure, many of you have been asking: which faith? One might agree that faith, in some sense of the term, is necessary to human life. But there are so many competing faiths that this general point does not solve our actual problem. Of course, I am convinced that just the recognition of our need for some kind of faith is a long first step. We cannot expect the capacity for critical judgment in an area of life which we have long ignored. We must first become convinced of the importance of searching for the truth in this realm. If we can attain the attitude of serious concern, this in itself will help to prevent us from being deceived by subhuman or irrational faiths. If we are fully serious about our need for faith, we will be critical, in the best sense of the term, about any particular faith. We will not accept anything which urges us, in the name of expediency or peace of mind, to blink at the facts or ignore what we do know about man and his peace in the world.

It is my own conviction that any faith which is worth being serious about and which is relevant to our dilemma will be found to be a *theocentric* faith. Perhaps modern man would not feel a dilemma at all if it were not for the fact that he sees clearly that a center of meaning and value for life must not be a purely private or subjective thing. If there is a good which is worthy of man's allegiance, it must not merely be the reflection of personal, group, or national interest. Modern man's passion for objectivity, nurtured in the school of science, makes him quick to suspect any faith which seems like special pleading. Yet his attempt to win objectivity of values by the same methods which proved successful in science has seemed to fail. He stands in danger, therefore, of concluding that there is no such thing as a center of meaning and value which is objective. It seems to me that a theocentric faith speaks to this situation. For it proclaims that there is a center of meaning and value, but it insists that it is not simply in the possession of any man or group of men. The meaning and value are grounded in God and, therefore, transcend the formulations of them which may be achieved by any special group. God, as the norm of meaning and value, cannot be identified with any man's or group's conception of God. A theocentric faith, that is to say, points ever beyond its own formulation. It contains within itself a dimension of depth which guards against dogmatism. It calls us to the worship not of the creed or of the church but of God. A theocentric faith is, on the one hand, a bulwark against meaninglessness and cynicism; for it points in faith to an ultimate meaning. It is, on the other hand, a bulwark against dogmatism and fanaticism; for it proclaims that this ultimate meaning is never simply centered in man or man's wisdom.

I have argued that the solution to man's dilemma is faith. But it must be a faith in a Reality which is active in judging particular formulations of the faith. Faith must point to God but never pretend to contain Him. This kind of faith is the creative element in human life by virtue of which alone we can get beyond the paralyzing dilemmas of reason and desire, without falling into the frenzy of fanaticism.

Occasionally we see this kind of faith exemplified so clearly in the life of a man that its lesson stands out more clearly than any words can convey. Since I have come to know about him, it has always seemed to me that Albert Schweitzer speaks to our time in just this way. Never was there a man who struggled more faithfully than he to know the truth, to know it with all the critical faculties of his mind and in the face of all the facts which science has presented to modern man. One of his most profound books, *The Quest of the Historical Jesus,* is an attempt to bring every technique of historical criticism and every bit of modern knowledge of history to bear upon the question: who and what was this man? In the end, Schweitzer felt that he had really failed. For no clear-cut and rational solution was forthcoming. He felt the same frustration in all his mighty questioning concerning religious doctrine and ethical systems. Yet behind all this he felt the creative urge to respond to what he somehow discerned as a meaning for all of life which transcended all that he could ever know. His learning did not paralyze his commitment. And, in the end, he felt that it was through his commitment that he attained a measure of understanding. The closing paragraph of his book provides not only a fitting close to this address but a fitting commentary upon the quality of Schweitzer's own life. He was speaking here of the Jesus whom he had sought to find by reason.

> He comes to us, as One unknown, without a name, as of old, by the lake-side, He came to those who knew Him not. He speaks to us the same word: "Follow thou Me!" and sets us to the tasks which He has to fulfill for our time. He commands. And to those who obey Him, whether they be wise or simple, He will reveal Himself in the toils, the conflicts, the sufferings which they shall pass through in His fellowship, and, as an ineffable mystery, they shall learn in their own experience Who He is.[9]

CHAPTER TWO

Existential Analyses
and
Religious Symbols

PAUL TILLICH

Charles A. Briggs Graduate Professor
of Philosophical Theology
Union Theological Seminary
(now Professor of Religion,
Harvard University)

Existential Analyses and Religious Symbols

EXISTENTIAL ANALYSES are older than existential philosophy. It is a familiar event in the history of philosophy that a special philosophy opens one's eyes to a special problem which was not unknown to former philosophers but which was not the center of their attention. If they or their followers then assert that this problem is nothing new for them, they are both right and wrong. They are right because most problems and perhaps even most types of solutions are as old as man's asking of the philosophical question. They are wrong because the movement of human thought is driven by the intensity with which old problems are seen in a new light and brought out of a peripheral significance into a central one. This is just what has happened to the existential problems. They were pushed into the background after the Renaissance and Reformation, definitely so following the victory of Cartesianism and theological rationalism. It was the function of the Existentialist movement to rediscover the significance of the existentialist questions and to reformulate them in the light of present day experiences and insights.

The thesis of this paper is that in the period during which the existential questions were pushed aside or forgotten, the cognitive approach to religious symbolism was largely blocked, and that the turning of many representatives of twentieth century philosophy, literature and

37

art to existential questions has once again opened the approach to religious symbols. For religious symbols are partly a way of stating the same situation with which existential analyses are concerned; partly they are answers to the questions implied in the situation. They are the former when they speak of man and his predicament. They are the latter when they speak of God and his reaction to this predicament. In both cases, existential analysis makes the religious symbols understandable and a matter of possible concern for our contemporaries, including contemporary philosophers.

In order to define the nature of an existential analysis we must distinguish it from an essential analysis. The terms "existential" and "essential" analyses shall be used here as grammatical abbreviations for analyses of existential structures and analyses of essential structures, while the terms "essentialist" and "existentialist" shall be used for the movements and attitudes of the one or the other character.

Since the analysis of existential structures is predominantly an analysis of the human predicament, the best way of distinguishing existential and essential analyses is to do so with respect to their doctrines of man. There is a large group of problems concerning man which have been investigated and discussed throughout the history of philosophy in purely essentialist terms. They all deal with the question, What is the "nature" of man? What is his *ousia*, that which makes him what he is, in every exemplar who deserves the name man? Neither nominalism nor process philosophy, neither philosophical empiricism nor even existentialism can escape this question. Attempts to describe human nature in its essential structures, be it

in more static or in more dynamic terms, can never cease
to be a task of human thought.

The existentialist philosopher, for example, asks the
question of the *differentia specifica* between man and non-
human nature. If he answers the question with Aristotle,
that man is *animal rationale*, this may not be specific
enough, or the nature of the rational may not have been
defined sufficiently, but the method itself is correct and
clearly essentialist. There are theologians who react vio-
lently against the Aristotelian definition, not in order to
amend it in this or that direction, but in order to deny
the method in the name of an assumedly existentialist
analysis of man's nature. They point to man's existential
relation to God and consider this relation as the nature
of man, misinterpreting for their purpose the Biblical
phrase that man is the image of God. In the Biblical
view, man is and always remains the image of God because
of his bodily and spiritual qualities which give him control
over nature in spite of his estrangement from his essential
being. This is an important point because its negation
was one of the ways by which neo-orthodox theology cut
off all relations with essentialist philosophy and surren-
dered all rational criteria for theological thought.

The question of man's essential nature leads by itself
to the mind-body problem. If we discuss the several
monistic and dualistic answers given to this ever-present
question and try to find a solution to it, we do an essentialist analysis. And we should reject theologians who
interfere in this discussion out of an existential interest.
They are aware of man's finitude and the question of the
infinite which is implicit in his finitude. And they try
to give an answer in terms of an essentialist psychology
which includes an immortal part of man. This is the

key to the failure of Thomas Aquinas when he tried to combine the essentialist Aristotelian doctrine of the soul as a form of the body with the Platonic-Christian dualism of the immortal soul and the mortal body. By this attempted combination, Aquinas injected existentialist analysis.

A third problem discussed in essentialist analyses of human nature is the relation of man as individuality and man as community. Again, the Aristotelian definition of man as a political animal is truly essentialist and remains valid, however it is enlarged upon or refined. Today the discussion of the problem is presented in Martin Buber's famous phrase, " the I-Thou relationship." This phrase *can* be understood in essentialist terms and can be used as a descriptive feature, showing how the ego becomes an ego only in the encounter with another ego in which it finds its limit and is thrown back upon itself. Therefore, man's ethical and cultural life is possible only in the community in which language is created. In this sense the ego-thou interdependence is a piece of essential analysis. Yet it was an existentialist invasion when Buber tried to remove the universals from the encounter between ego and thou, and to make both speechless, because there are no words for the absolute particular, the other ego. And it was a distortion of communal being when Heidegger referred to the problem as an escape into the non-authentic form of being, the being as a " *man* " (German), as an " *on* " (French), as a general " one." The political body of which Aristotle speaks is not the result of an escape into unauthentic being. Essentialism is right in rejecting this as an invasion.

A last example is man's ethical structure. Essentialist analysis has described it either in terms of the formal

categories which constitute the ethical realm, as, for example, Kant did, or in terms of the ethical character and
its virtues, as, for example, in the manner of Aquinas,
or in terms of the embracing social structures, as, for
example, according to Hegel. Kierkegaard has accused
Hegel of neglecting man's ethical situation, namely, that
of the individual who has to make the ethical decision.
But although Hegel obviously neglects the structures which
make the singular person as such a moral subject, he
cannot be accused of excluding in his essentialist analyses
the existentialist question, the question of the anxiety of
decision to which Kierkegaard refers. If neo-orthodox
theologians deny that the Bible has essentialist ethical
material in the manner of Aristotle and the Stoics, they
can be refuted not only by the partly Stoic elements of
the Pauline letters, but also by the fact that the content of
the ethical law never has been denied in the New Testament. Only its character as law is denied for those who are
reconciled unto themselves. There can be no ethics without an essentialist analysis of man's ethical nature and its
structures.

We have given examples of essentialist analyses of man's
nature as they have been performed in all periods of
philosophical thought. At the same time, we have drawn
attention to existentialist attacks on this kind of philos-
ophizing and to the necessity on our part of rejecting these
attacks. In doing so, we have given first indications of
what an existentialist analysis is, namely, a description
of man's anti-essential or estranged predicament. We have
also indicated that the existentialist attacks to which we
have referred have continuously interfered with the essentialist task.

If we now turn to a more direct characterization of

existential analyses, we find that in contrast to essentialism they concentrate on the human situation and that their point of departure is the immediate awareness man has of his situation. Both characteristics follow from what an existential analysis is supposed to do, namely, to describe those elements within experience which express being in contrast to what it essentially is. This experience is not a matter of objectifying observation from outside the situation. It can be understood only as an immediate awareness from inside the situation. It has, for example, the character of finitude itself in contrast to a finitude which I see objectively if something comes to an end. One may think here of the difference between the observed death of someone else and the anticipation of one's own death. In the first experience, the material of an essential analysis is given; in the second experience, one's existential situation is manifested in anxiety. Another example is the experience of guilt. It is an essentialist analysis if types of law-breakers are described or the degree of guilt in a criminal action is discussed. But guilt becomes an existentialist concept if it is the expression of one's own deviation from what one essentially is and therefore ought to be. Guilt in this sense is connected with the anxiety of losing one's true being.

A third example is provided by the experience of meaninglessness. We often have the more or less adequate impression that somebody lives an empty and meaningless life, without being fully aware of his doing so. Quite different from such an essential description is the experience of feeling oneself cut off from any meaning of life, of being lost in a desert of meaninglessness and of feeling the anxiety implicit in this situation.

In each of these examples, to which others will be added

later on, I alluded to what I suggest calling "existential anxiety." This points to the fact that the concept of anxiety has played a decisive role in all existentialist thinking since Augustine and Pascal. I assume that the frequently discussed distinction between anxiety and fear is known and largely accepted. The main point is that fear has a definite object and is, as such, an object of essentialist philosophy, while anxiety has no definite object and is a matter of existential analysis. With this thought in mind, I want to draw your attention to some symbols of anxiety in literature. Dante's descriptions of the Inferno must be understood as structures of destruction in man's existential experience of estrangement, guilt and despair. They symbolize modes of despair as external punishments. Taken literally, they are absurd as are the symbols in Kafka's novels *The Castle* and *The Trial*. In the first instance, symbols of the anxiety of meaninglessness are given; in the second case, symbols of the anxiety of guilt. Conceptualized or symbolized, the description of anxiety is central for the existential attitude.

In order to give further examples of existential analyses, I want to reverse the procedure which I first used: that is, I shall cite essentialist criticisms of existential analyses and then the existential defense against the criticisms.

Essentialism criticizes the existentialist emphasis on anxiety and related concepts by denying that there is a qualitative difference between them and other internal experiences. The so-called existential analyses, are, so it is said, essential analyses of a predominantly psychological character. Experienced anxiety is like experienced anger or sadness or joy, an object of the psychology of emotions, a part of the general description of human nature. It is claimed that nothing verifiable in existential analyses is included in any essentialist description. If these arguments are valid, the existentialist claim has been refuted. But they are not valid. For there is a sharp qualitative difference between two kinds of affections (in the Cartesian-Spinozistic sense of affections). The one kind belongs to man's essential nature and embraces the totality of those affections which respond to stimuli coming from the universe of objects in the temporal-spatial continuum. Most of the affections discussed in ancient and modern philosophy have this character. They are objects of essentialist psychological descriptions.

But there is another kind, namely, those which respond to man's existence as existence and not to any stimuli coming from the contents man encounters within existence. Being aware of existence, experiencing it as existence, means being in anxiety. For existence includes finitude, and anxiety is the awareness of one's own finitude.

I have already pointed to the difference between fear and anxiety, the first having an object, the second not having one. But we must go one step further. Anxiety is the more fundamental affection because the fear of something special is ultimately rooted in the fact that as finite beings we are exposed to annihilation, to the victory of non-being in us. In this sense, anxiety is the foundation of fear. Their ontological relation is different; for anxiety has an ontological precedence; it reveals the human predicament in its fundamental quality, as finitude.

The relation of anxiety to fear is representative of similar relations in which two partly synonymous concepts point to something qualitatively different, the one to an essential structure, the other to an existential characteristic.

Since a comprehensive treatment of existential analysis is obviously impossible on this occasion, I shall restrict myself to those aspects of it which are especially useful as keys to the meaning of religious symbols.

Man in his existential anxiety feels estranged from that to which he properly belongs. Although created by Hegel in order to make the fact of nature understandable from the point of view of the absolute mind, the term soon acquired an existentialist meaning and has, since then, been used against Hegel. Man feels estranged from what he essentially is; he experiences a permanent conflict within himself and a hostility towards the world. This must be distinguished, though not separated, from the feeling of strangeness which every living being, animal as well as man, has for most of the other beings and often for himself. The emotions of strangeness and its opposite, familiarity, belong to the realm of essential relationships between finite beings. But estrangement is a negation of essential belongingness. It has an existential character.

Existential estrangement expresses itself in loneliness, which should be clearly distinguished from essential solitude, the correlate of which is essential community. Loneliness is an expression of anti-essential separation from that to which one belongs. This loneliness can express itself in the flight from solitude into the " on," the " man."

Finitude includes insecurity. There is essential insecurity, the correlate to essential security, in the biological, social, and psychological realm. In all these spheres risk and chance are at work, but also law and certainty. The contrast to that is the ultimate insecurity of existence which is experienced in anxiety and described as being homeless and lost in one's world, and as being anxious about tomorrow, in German, sorgen. The distinction between being anxious and taking care, between Sorge and *Vorsorge,* is again linguistic support for the distinction between an essentialist and an existentialist concept. Essential insecurity may provoke the feeling of ultimate insecurity; but conversely, in an externally secure situation, existential insecurity may come as a sudden shock as it breaks into the world of finite relations.

The anxiety of estrangement has the color of existential guilt. We have already spoken of " guilt " as an example of the difference between an essential and an existential analysis. This distinction must be carried through in several directions. The first is the establishment of the existentialist concept of risk or of daring decision. In every decision a risk is implied; the risk to win or to lose something or someone. This belongs to man's essential character or finite freedom. He deliberates and then risks a decision. He may even risk his life. But there is another risk which belongs to man which is the cause of guilt and estrangement, namely, the risk of actualizing or non-actualizing himself, and in doing so to lose himself, namely, his essential being. This situation can be observed in every moment in which innocence is put before the decision either to remain in a state of non-actualized potentialities or to trespass the state of innocence and to actualize them. In both cases, something is lost; in the first, a fully actualized humanity; in the second, the innocent resting in mere potentiality. The classical example is the sexual anxiety of the adolescent.

As myth and experience tell, mankind as a whole risks its self-actualization and is consequently in the state of universal, existential estrangement. This produces the situation of tragic guilt in which everyone, in spite of his personal responsibility, participates. An early philosophical expression of this experience of being involved by destiny in a universal situation for which one is at the same time responsible seems to be the fragment of Anaximander, which, however one interprets particulars, combines separation, finitude, and guilt in a cosmic vision. This certainty transcends an essentialist analysis of responsible or irresponsible actions between persons. It judges the predicament of man and his world as such.

The last confrontation of an essentialist and an existentialist concept concerns man's cognitive estrangement from his essential being, as it is manifest in the situation of doubt. Doubt in the form of finite freedom is an essential element in the cognitive task of man. Essential doubt is the condition of all knowledge. The methodological doubt of Descartes was the entering door for the modern scientific consciousness. Quite different from it is the existential doubt, the doubt about the meaning of one's being in man's existential situation. Essential doubt is an expression of courage; existential doubt is a cause and an expression of despair. It is doubt neither of special assertions nor of all possible assertions, but it is the doubt about the meaning of being. It is the doubt concerning the being of him who doubts. It turns against itself and against the doubter and his world. And since it wrestles with the threat of meaninglessness, it cannot be answered by any of those assertions which have methodological certainty, probability, or improbability.

These are examples of existential analyses which seem to me sufficient to show the qualitative difference and independent standing of existential concepts and which may also be used as keys for the interpretation of religious symbols.

The examples we have given to show the difference between existential and essential analyses have provided

47

us with the material necessary to interpret the basic religious symbols. It is almost a truism to assert that religious language is symbolic. But it is less of a truism to assert that for this reason religious language expresses the truth, the truth which cannot be expressed and communicated in any other language. And it is far from a truism to say that most errors in religion and most attacks on religion are due to the confusion between symbolic and literal language. This confusion, which must remain a chief concern of everyone who takes religion seriously, is not only a failure of the intellect, but also a symptom of the idolatrous distortion which is found in all religions and which makes the divine an object amongst objects to be handled by man as subject, cognitively and practically.

Once this fact is understood, one can easily see the relation between existential analyses and religious symbols. Existential analyses express conceptually what the religious myth has always said about the human predicament. And in doing so they make all of those symbols understandable in which the answer to the question implied in the human predicament is given: the symbols and myths which center around the idea of God.

Existential analysis deals with man's finitude as it is experienced in anxiety. The mythological symbol for this experience is man as a creature. Man and his world are creatures. Some forms of this symbol can be found in every religion. Man is not by himself. He has not what God has in classical theology, *aseitas*. He is a mixture of contrasting elements, divine and demonic, spiritual and material, heavenly and earthly, being and non-being. This is true of Eastern as well as Western religions, although the difference between the two appears immediately if one asks for the meaning of creaturely existence. The answer given in the East is negative and non-historical. Creaturely existence is something which should not be and from which one desires to be saved. In the West, the answer is positive and historical. There should be creaturely existence, but it must be saved not from itself as creature, but from its self-estrangement.

The consequence of the Western attitude is that creation has a positive side, answering the question implied in the experience of creatureliness. The answer is not a story according to which once upon a time a divine or half-divine being decided to produce other things. But creation expresses symbolically the participation of the finite in its own infinite ground; or, more existentially expressed, the symbol of creation shows the source of the courage to affirm one's own being in terms of power and meaning in spite of the ever present threat of non-being. In this courage, the anxiety of creatureliness is not removed but taken into the courage. And in it, the loneliness of the estranged individual is taken into a unity which does not remove the threat of loneliness and its correlate, the flight into the " man," the " on," but which instead is able to create genuine solitude and genuine communion. And in the symbol of creation, existential insecurity is taken into a certitude which does not remove the insecurity of having no definite time and no definite space but which instead gives the security of participation in the ultimate power of being. Symbols like omnipotence, omnipresence, and providence corroborate this meaning. They become absurdities and contradictions if taken literally. They radiate existential truth if opened up with the key of existential analysis.

In the center of the symbolism of many religions we find the contrast of the fall and salvation together with a large group of corroborating symbols. The key to existential analysis is able to open them up even for those who have a special strong resistance against this kind of symbolism.

The symbolism of temptation has already been mentioned in connection with the analysis of the anxiety of existential decisions. Temptation is possibility, and the anxiety of having to decide is the awareness of possibility. There are many myths and legends of temptation of which probably the most profound is the Biblical story in which the situation of man, symbolized by Adam and Eve, is clearly the decision between remaining in the dreaming innocence of Paradise and achieving self-realization in knowledge, power, and sex. Man chooses self-realization and falls into the state of estrangement, and with him his world also falls. Understood in this way, the myth of the fall, for which there are analogies in most religions, represents a very particular case of the transition from the innocence of potentiality to the tragic guilt of self-actualization. It is a genuine description of man's predicament here and now and should not be vitiated by the absurdities of literalism.

The traditional term for man's status of estrangement is " sin," a term whose meaning has undergone more distortions and has consequently been the object of more protest than almost any other religious notion. Sin, in the light of existential analysis, is man's estrangement from his essential being, an estrangement which is both tragic necessity and personal guilt. The extremely questionable terms " original sin " and " hereditary sin " express the tragic and actual sin, the personal element. I suggest that we drop the terms " original sin " and " hereditary sin " completely. They seem to be beyond salvation. And certainly some words, especially theological and philosophical ones, need salvation. The term " original sin " should be replaced by existential descriptions of the universal and tragic character of man's estrangement. But the term can and should be saved by being reinterpreted as the stage of estrangement for which, in spite of its tragic character, we are personally responsible and out of which the concrete acts of estrangement from ourselves, from others, and from the meaning of our being, follow. If we use the term "sin," it should not be used in the plural but in the singular, without the article, as Paul does: sin, the power of estrangement.

The state of estrangement is the state in which the anxiety of guilt is amalgamated with the anxiety of finitude. The predominant religious symbols of this anxiety are, as already indicated in relation to Dante's poem, judgment, condemnation, punishment, and hell. They usually appear in a dramatic framework with a divine being as judge, demonic powers as executors, and a special place reserved for long-lasting or everlasting punishment. Although this imagery is largely recognized as such even in the average membership of the Christian churches, it is good to apply here also the keys of existential and depth-psychological analyses. It seems that in people like Peter Brueghel this was already a conscious situation. His highly existential pictures of the demonic realm are understandable only in the light of an existential analysis of the anxiety of guilt. Seen in this light, the divine law, according to which judgment is executed, is obviously the law of one's essential being, judging us because of the estrangement from ourselves. Only because of this situation has the law as law an unconditional character, however the content of the law may change. Seen in this light, condemnation and punishment are obviously not things which judge us from above, but symbols of the judgment we inescapably make against ourselves, of the painful split within ourselves, of the moments of despair in which we want to get rid of ourselves without being able to, of the feeling of being possessed by structures of self-destruction, in short, of all of that which the myth calls demonic.

The question and perhaps the passionate quest included in this situation is mythologically expressed in symbols such as salvation, redemption, regeneration, and justification, or in personal symbols such as savior, mediator, Messiah, Christ. Such symbols are common to most of the great religions, although the description of the way of salvation is immensely different.

Existential analyses have given decisive keys for the understanding of this symbolism, the dramatic frame of which corresponds to the dramatic frame of the symbols of estrangement. Some of these keys merit special mention. The first is connected with a semantic reflection by means of which salvation makes a whole of something which is split. *Salvus* and *saos* mean whole and healed. Salvation is the act in which the cleavage between man's essential being and his existential situation is overcome. It is the religious answer to the innumerable analyses which can be summed up in the title of Menninger's book *Man Against Himself.* The second key is equally prepared by existential analysis, namely, the insight that the situation of existence cannot be overcome in the power of this situation. Every attempt to do so strengthens this situation, which can be summed up in the title of Sartre's play, *No Exit.* That is how the religious symbols which point to saving powers in non-personal and personal embodiments must be understood. The tragic bondage of estranged existence produces the quest for that which transcends existence although it appears within it, creating a new being. This and this alone is the religious paradox and not simply a logically " nonsense-ical " statement. The third key which has been successfully used is the understanding of reconciliation in the light of the experience of methodological as well as poetic-intuitive psychology. It is the idea that the most difficult thing for a human being is to accept himself and that the basic step in the process of healing is to give man the feeling that he *is* accepted and therefore can accept himself. Nobody understands today what justification by faith means. Everyone understands what it means to accept oneself as accepted.

In the analysis of existential doubt, in contrast to essential doubt, we touched on the concept of despair, literally, of hopelessness. Existentialist thinking, especially at one period of its development, devoted a great deal of work to the problem of nihilism, meaninglessness, nothingness, etc. The wide spread of this feeling is confirmed by many witnesses in this country as well as in Europe. Its analysis gives a key to a long neglected part of religious symbolism, the symbols of hope. Most religions are full of mythological, usually very fanciful, images of hope. Taken literally in any sense, they appear as pale but beautified images of our daily experienced world. Taken as highly symbolical, they express the conviction that in the realities of our daily experience, in spite of their seemingly meaningless transitoriness and ultimate emptiness, there is a dimension of meaning which points to an ultimate or external meaning in which they participate here and now. This is the key to the symbol of eternal life which can be more easily used in such an interpretation because it is less open to literalism than more dramatic but dangerously inadequate symbols such as life after death, immortality, reincarnation, heaven. Eternal life means that the joy of today has a dimension which gives it trans-temporal meaning.

In each of our attempts to open up a religious symbol with the help of an existential analysis, we open up implicitly the basic and all-embracing symbol of religion, namely the symbol of God. In relation to creation, He is creator; in relation to salvation, He is savior; in relation to fulfillment, He is the eternal. We lead from different points and with different keys to the central symbol. But we do not start with it. This is an implication of the existential method, which, I believe, is adequate to religion, because religion is a matter of man's existential situation. We must start from below and not from above. We must start with man's experienced predicament and the questions implied in it; and we must proceed to the symbols which claim to contain the answer. But we must not start with the question of the being of God, which, if discussed in terms of the existence or non-existence of God, is in itself a lapse into a disastrous literalism.

Following the method which goes from below to above, we reach an idea of God which avoids literalism and which, just for this reason, establishes the reality of that which answers the questions implied in human existence. God, in the light of this question, is the power of being itself, prevailing over against non-being, overcrowding estrangement, providing us the courage to take the anxiety of finitude, guilt, and doubt upon ourselves. This experience is expressed in innumerable largely personal symbols describing the idea of God. Symbols are not signs. They participate in the power of what they symbolize. They are not true or false in the sense of cognitive judgments. But they are authentic or inauthentic with respect to their rise; they are adequate or inadequate with respect to their expressive power; they are divine or demonic with respect to their relation to the ultimate power of being.

The vast problem of symbols, however, lies beyond the scope of the present discussion. My task was to show that existential analysis has made it more difficult for the modern mind to dispose of religious symbols by first taking them literally and then properly rejecting them as absurd. Any attack on symbolism must be conducted on a much deeper level, namely that of symbolism itself. Genuine symbols can be overcome only by other genuine symbols, not by criticism of their literalistic distortions.

CHAPTER THREE

The Biblical View
of
Reality

ABRAHAM J. HESCHEL

*Associate Professor of Jewish Ethics
and Mysticism, Jewish Theological
Seminary of America*

The Biblical View
of Reality

PHILOSOPHY of religion is primarily not the philosophy of a philosophy, the philosophy of a doctrine, the interpretations of a dogma, but the philosophy of concrete events, acts, insights, of that which is immediately given with the pious man. The dogmas are merely a catalog, an indispensable index. For religion is more than a creed or an ideology and cannot be understood when detached from actual living. It comes to light in moments in which one's soul is shaken with unmitigated concern about the meaning of all meaning, about one's ultimate commitment which is integrated with his very existence; in moments in which all foregone conclusions, all life-stifling trivialities are suspended, in which the soul is starved for an inkling of eternal reality; in moments of discerning the indestructibly sudden within the perishably constant.[1]

Thus the issue which must be discussed first is not belief, ritual, or the religious experience, but the source of these phenomena: the total situation of man; not what or how he experiences the supernatural, but why he experiences and accepts it. What necessitates religion in my life and yours?

In our quest of an answer it is important to inquire: What was the source of the faith of the people of the Bible? Is it correct to define their faith as an act of relying upon an inherited doctrine? Is it correct to say that the records of revelation were the only direct source of faith, or that Judaism derived its religious vitality exclusively from loyalty to the events that happened in the days of Moses and from obedience to Scripture in which those events were recorded? Such an assumption seems to overlook the nature of man and his faith. A great event, miraculous as it may be, if it happened only once, will hardly be able to dominate forever the minds of men. The mere remembrance of such an event is too weak to hold in its spell the soul of man with its restlessness and vitality. There must have been a continuous stream out of which Jewish faith was drawn.

The prophets appeal to the spiritual power in man: " Know therefore this day, and lay it to your heart, that the Lord is God in heaven above and on the earth beneath; there is no other " (Deuteronomy 4:39). The Psalmist calls upon us: " O *taste* and see that the Lord is good " (34:9).[2] How does one know? How does one taste?

Indeed, the belief of the people of Israel was not an act of blind acceptance of dogmas but rather the result of insight, the outcome of their being exposed to the power and presence of God in the world.

There is in the Bible God's word to man, but there is also man's word to God; man's insight, not only God's approach. To recapture that insight is to delve into the inside of the religious drama of Israel, to grasp what it was that enabled Job to say:

> As for me, I know that my Redeemer lives,
> that He will witness at the last upon the dust.
> After my skin has been destroyed,
> from my flesh I shall see God.
> My own eyes shall behold, not another's.
> My heart faints within me.

> —Job 19:25-27

Yet how does a man reach a stage of thinking where he could "see God from his flesh"? What are the ways that lead to the certainty of this existence, to the perception of His presence?

The Bible contains within its words the answer to our questions. Yet that answer is rarely spelled out, and we must learn to ascertain the reasons for that certainty, the perception behind the utterance. This means going to the roots of Biblical experience and asking: Is there anything within the world that would enable us to sense the existence and presence of Him who creates the world? To answer this question we must first ask: What is the world to the Biblical man?

There are three aspects of nature that command man's attention: *power, loveliness, grandeur.* Power he exploits, loveliness he enjoys, grandeur fills him with awe. It is according to how deeply man is drawn to one of these aspects that his particular way of knowledge is developed. Western knowledge of the last four centuries may be characterized by the famous principle of Bacon: *knowledge is power.* The goal of that knowledge is neither to portray the beauty nor to convey the grandeur of the world, but to exploit its resources. Man, proud to be *homo faber*, regards the world as a source of satisfaction of his needs. He is willing to define his essence as "a seeker after the greatest degree of comfort for the least necessary expenditure of energy." His hero is the technician rather than the artist, the philosopher, or the prophet. Out of such a system of knowledge it is hard to find a way to the reality of God. Nature as power is a world that does not point beyond itself. It is when nature is sensed as mystery and grandeur that it calls upon us to look beyond it. Similarly, when nature is sensed as beauty, we become infatuated

61

by her grace and look to her for answers to problems she is incapable of giving. It is when nature is sensed as mystery and grandeur that we discover that nature herself is the problem.

Significantly, the theme of Biblical poetry is not the charm or beauty of nature; it is the *sublime* aspect of nature which is constantly referred to.

What was the world, what was reality to the Biblical man? The Hebrew word *'olam* that in post-Biblical times came to denote the world is, according to many scholars, derived from the root *'alam*, which means to hide, to conceal.[3] The world is hiddenness; its essence is mystery. In the Bible, where the word *'olam* expresses a conception of time, the world is never taken for granted or regarded as an instrument of the human will.

In awe and amazement the prophets stand before the mystery of the universe:

> Who has measured the waters in the hollow of his
>   hand,
> And marked off the heavens with a span,
> Enclosed the dust of the earth in a measure,
> And weighed the mountains in scales,
> And the hills in a balance?
>
> —Isaiah 40:12

An even deeper sense of humility is expressed in the words of Agur:

> Surely I am too stupid to be a man.
> I have not the understanding of a man.
> I have not learned wisdom,
> Nor have I knowledge of the Holy One.
> Who has ascended to heaven and come down?
> Who has gathered the wind in his fists?

Who has wrapped up the waters in a garment?
Who has established all the ends of the earth?
What is his name, and what is his son's name,
If thou knowest?

—Proverbs 30:2-4

Such an attitude toward the mystery and grandeur of nature affected, of course, the Biblical understanding of the meaning and scope of human knowledge and wisdom.

Philosophy is the love and quest of wisdom. To attain wisdom is one of the highest aspirations.

But where shall wisdom be found?
Where is the place of understanding?
Man does not know the way to it;
It is not found in the land of the living.
The deep says, " It is not in me ";
The sea says, " It is not with me. . . ."
Whence then comes wisdom?
And where is the place of understanding?
It is hidden from the eyes of all living,
And concealed from the birds of the air.
Destruction and Death say,
" We have heard a rumor of it with our ears."
God understands the way to it,
He knows its place.
For He looks to the ends of the earth,
And sees everything under the heavens.
When He gave to the wind its weight,
And meted out the waters by measure;
When He made a decree for the rain,
And a way for the lightning of the thunder;
Then He saw it and declared it;
He established it, and searched it out.
And He said to man,

"Behold, the fear of the Lord, that is wisdom;
And to depart from evil is understanding."

—Job 28:12-14, 20-28

In another book of the Bible, in Ecclesiastes, we read the account of a man who sought wisdom, who searched for insight into the world and its meaning. " I said, I will be wise " (7:23) and " I applied my mind to know wisdom and to see what is done on earth " (8:16). Did he succeed? He claims, " I have acquired great wisdom, surpassing all who were over Jerusalem before me " (1:16). And yet, he ultimately realized " that *man cannot find out* the work that is done under the sun. However much man may toil in seeking, he will not find it out; even though a wise man claims to know, he cannot find it out " (8:17).

" I said, *I will be wise,* but it was far from me. *That which is is far off and deep, exceeding deep. Who can find it out?* " (7:23-24). Ecclesiastes is not only saying that " the world's wise are not wise," but something more radical. What *is* is more than what you see; what is is " far off and deep, exceeding deep." *Being is mysterious.*

This is one of Ecclesiastes' central insights: " I have seen the task that God has given to the sons of men. . . . He has made everything beautiful in its time; but He has *also implanted in* the hearts of men *the mystery,* so that man cannot find out what God has done from the beginning to the end " (3:10-11).

Wisdom is beyond our reach. We are unable to attain insight into the ultimate meaning and purpose of things. Man does not even know the thoughts of his own mind; nor is he able to understand the meaning of his own dreams. (See Daniel 2:27.)

These are the last words in the Book of Job:

Who is this that hides counsel without knowledge?
Therefore have I uttered what I did not understand,
Things too wonderful for me, which I did not know.
Hear, and I will speak;
I will question you, and you declare to me.
I had heard of Thee by the hearing of the ear;
But now my eye sees Thee;
Therefore I despise myself, and repent in dust and
    ashes.

—Job 42:3-6

What have Job, Agur, Ecclesiastes discovered in their search? They have discovered that the existence of the world is a most mysterious fact. Referring not to miracles, to startling phenomena, but to the natural order of things, they insist that the world of the known is a world unknown, of hiddenness, of mystery. Not the apparent but the hidden is the apparent; not the order but the mystery of the order that prevails in the universe is what man is called upon to behold. The prophet, like Job and Agur, alludes to a reality that discredits our wisdom, that shatters our knowledge. It is the mystery where we start from without presuppositions, without allegations, without doctrines, without dogmas.

Spencer and others " seem to be possessed with the idea that science has got the universe pretty well ciphered down to a fine point; while the Faradays and Newtons seem to themselves like children who have picked up a few pretty pebbles upon the ocean beach. But most of us find it difficult to recognize the greatness and wonder of things familiar to us. As the prophet is not without honor save [in his own country] so it is also with phenomena." [4]

The Biblical man had not forfeited his sense of radical amazement. That " wonder is the feeling of a philosopher, and that philosophy begins in wonder " was stated by Plato [5] and maintained by Aristotle: " For it is owing to their wonder that men both now being and at first began to philosophize." [6] To this day, wonder is appreciated as *semen scientiae*, the seed of knowledge, as something conducive to cognition, not indigenous to it. Wonder is the prelude to knowledge; it ceases, once the cause of a phenomenon is explained.[7]

But does the worth of wonder merely consist in its being a stimulant to the acquisition of knowledge? Is wonder the same as curiosity? To the prophets wonder is a form of thinking; it never ceases. There is no answer in the world to ultimate amazement.[8]

> Who is like Thee, O Lord, among the gods?
> Who is like Thee, majestic in holiness,
> Terrible in glorious deeds, doing wonders?
>
> —Exodus 15:11

> Wonderful are Thy works,
> And my soul knows it exceedingly.
>
> —Psalms 139:14

> Many things has Thou done, O Lord my God,
> Even Thy wondrous deeds and Thy thoughts toward us.
> There is nothing to be compared unto Thee!
> If I would declare and speak of them,
> They are more than can be told.
>
> —Psalms 40:6

What is so wondrous about the world? What is there in reality that evokes supreme awe in the hearts of man? In his great vision Isaiah perceives the voice of the sera-

66

phim even before he hears the voice of the Lord. What is it that the seraphim reveal to Isaiah? *"The whole earth is full of His glory"* (6:3). It is proclaimed not as a Messianic promise but as a present fact. Man may not sense it, but the seraphim announce it. It is not to Isaiah only that this fact is the essential part of his revelation. Ezekiel, too, when the heavens were opened by the river Chebar, hears the voice of a great rushing, while cherubim cry, "Blessed be the glory of the Lord from His place" (3:12).

Is the glory a secret of the angels? According to the Psalmist, *"The heavens declare the glory of God"* (19:2). How do they declare it? "Day unto day utters *speech*, and night unto night reveals *knowledge*." Speech? Knowledge? What is the language, what are the words in which the heavens express the glory? *"There is no speech, there are no words, neither is their voice heard. . . ."* And yet: "Their line goes out through all the earth, and their words to the end of the world." The song of the heavens is *ineffable*.

Is the glory something that is seen, heard or clearly apprehended? In the same vision in which the ubiquity of the glory is proclaimed, there is an intimation of man's suspended sensibility.

> Go, and say to the people:
> "Hear and hear, but do not understand;
> See and see, but do not perceive."
> Make the heart of this people fat,
>   and their ears heavy
>   and shut their eyes;
> Lest they see with their eyes,
>   and hear with their ears,
> And understand with their hearts,
>   and turn and be healed.
>
> —Isaiah 6:9-10

The glory is visible, but we do not perceive it; it is within our reach, beyond our grasp.

> Lo, He passes by me, and I see Him not;
> He moves on, but I do not perceive Him.
>
> —Job 9:11

And still, the glory is not entirely unknown to us. That not only the heavens are able to declare it may be seen from the fact that the people are called upon to:

> Declare His glory among the nations,
> His marvels among all the peoples.
> —I Chronicles 16:24 (See also Psalms 145:5.)

When " the voice of the Lord breaks the cedars . . . flashes forth flames of fire . . . shakes the wilderness . . ." then " in His temple all cry ' Glory ' " (Psalms 29:9). It is, again, not an utterance in words. " The glory of God is to conceal words " (" a word," Proverbs 25:2).

What should be worshipped, what should be adored? Is there anything more than the world, more than what we see? Is not the world the end of perception and hence the only and ultimate object of adoration? It is hard to live under a sky full of stars and not be struck by its mystery. The sun is equipped with power and beauty for all eyes to see. Yet who could refrain from extolling its grandeur? Who could go beyond the realization that nature is the ultimate mystery? And is mystery the end?

It is natural for man to adore the great facts of nature, despite the injunction, " Beware lest you lift up your eyes to heaven, and when you see the sun and the moon and the stars, all the host of heaven, you be drawn away and worship them " (Deuteronomy 4:19). There were even in the times of the Babylonian Exile those who

turned their faces to the east and worshipped the sun.
(Ezekiel 8:16; compare II Kings 17:16, 21:3.)

Indeed, the beauty of nature is a menace to our spiritual
understanding; there is a deadly risk of being enchanted
by its power.

> If I have looked at the sun when it shone,
> Or the moon moving in splendor,
> And my heart has been secretly enticed,
> And my mouth has kissed my hand;
> This also would be an iniquity to be punished by the
>   judges,
> For I should have been false to God above.
>
> —Job 31:26-28

" To commune with the heart of Nature—this has been
the accredited mode since the days of Wordsworth. Nature,
Coleridge assures us, has ministrations by which she heals
her erring and distempered child. . . .

" Well, she is a very lovely Nature; . . . yet I confess a
heinous doubt whether rustic stolidity may not be a secret
effluence from her. You speak, and you think she answers
you. It is the echo of your own voice. You think you hear
the throbbing of her heart, and it is the throbbing of your
own. I do not believe that Nature has a heart; and I
suspect that, like many another beauty, she has been
credited with a heart because of her face. You go to her,
this great, beautiful, tranquil, self-satisfied Nature, and
you look for—sympathy? Yes; the sympathy of a cat, sitting
by the fire and blinking at you. What, indeed, does she
want with a heart or brain? She knows that she is beautiful, and she is placidly content with the knowledge; she
was made to be gazed on, and she fulfills the end of her
creation. After a careful anatomization of Nature, I pro-

nounce that she has nothing more than a lymphatic vesicle. She cannot give what she does not need; and if we were but similarly organized, we should be independent of sympathy. A man cannot go straight to his objects, because he has a heart; he cannot eat, drink, sleep, make money, and be satisfied, because he has a heart. It is a mischievous thing, and wise men accordingly take the earliest opportunity of giving it away.

" Yet the thing is, after all, too deep for jest. What is this heart of Nature, if it exist at all? Is it, according to the conventional doctrine derived from Wordsworth and Shelley, a heart of love, according with the heart of man, and stealing out to him through a thousand avenues of mute sympathy? No; in this sense I repeat seriously what I said lightly: Nature has no heart." [9]

Is the cosmos an object worthy of our adoration? The Bible's answer is: No! The whole world utters adoration; the whole world worships Him. Join all things in their song to Him. The world's beauty and power are as naught compared to Him. The mystery is only the beginning.

Beyond the mystery is God.

The Biblical man does see nature not in isolation but in relation to God. " At the beginning God created heaven and earth." These few words set forth the contingency and absolute dependence of all of reality. What, then, is reality? To the Western man, it is *a thing in itself*; to the Biblical man, it is *a thing through God.* Looking at a thing his eyes see not so much form, color, force and motion as an act of God. It is a way of seeing which has fortunately not vanished from the world.

I assert, for myself, that I do not behold the outward creation, and to me it is hindrance and not action. " What! " it will be questioned, " When the sun rises, do you not see a round disc of fire somewhat like a guinea?" Oh, no, no! I see an innumerable company of the heavenly host, crying, "Holy, holy, holy is the Lord God Almighty!" I question not my corporeal eye any more than I would question a window concerning a sight. I look through it, and now with it.[10]

Few are the songs in the Bible that celebrate the beauty of nature, and these songs are ample testimony to the fact that the Biblical man was highly sensitive to form, color, force and motion. And yet, because the link between the world and God was not broken in his mind, the beauty of the universe was not the supreme object of his adoration. To the Biblical man, the beauty of the world issued from the grandeur of God; His majesty towered beyond the breath-taking mystery of the universe. Rather than being crushed by the mystery, man was inspired to praise the majesty. And rather than praise the world for its beauty, he called upon the world to praise its creator.

What the Psalmist felt in meeting the world is succinctly expressed in the exclamation:

Sing unto the Lord a new song;
Sing unto the Lord, all the earth.

—Psalms 96:1

Praise Him, sun and moon,
Praise Him, all you shining stars!
Praise Him, you highest heavens,
And you waters above the heavens. . . .
Praise the Lord from the earth,
You sea-monsters and all deeps,
Fire and hail, snow and frost,
Stormy wind fulfilling His command!
Mountains and all hills,

71

Fruit trees and all cedars!
Beasts and all cattle,
Creeping things and flying birds!

—Psalms 148:3-9

The Egyptian priest could not call upon the stars to praise the gods. He believed that the soul of Isis sparkled in Sirius, the soul of Horus in Orion, and the soul of Typhon in the Great Bear; it was beyond his scope to conceive that all beings stand in awe and worship God. To the Biblical mind the soul of everything that lives blesses His name. " All Thy works praise Thee " (Psalms 145:10). Whose ear has ever heard how all trees sing to God? Has our reason ever thought of calling upon the sun to praise the Lord? And yet, what the ear fails to perceive, what reason fails to conceive, the Bible makes clear to our souls. It is a higher truth, to be grasped by the spirit.

Greek philosophy began in a world without God. It could not accept the gods or the example of their conduct. Plato had to break with the gods and to ask: What is good? And the problem of values was born. And it was the idea of values that took the place of God. Plato lets Socrates ask: What is good? Yet Moses' question was: What does God require of thee?

The argument from design, expounded in Cicero's *De Natura Deorum*, infers the existence of a divine power from the purposeful structure of nature. Order implies intelligence. That intelligence is God. A classic formulation is found in a familiar passage in Paley's *Natural Theology* (1803), chapter 1: " Suppose I had found a watch upon the ground. . . . The mechanism being observed. . . . The inference we think is inevitable that the watch must have a maker; that there must have existed, at some time, and at some place or other, an artificer or artificers, who formed it for the purpose which we find it actually to answer; who comprehended its construction, and designed its use."

The universe stands to God in the relation in which a watch is related to the mechanic who constructed it. The heavens are the works of His hands, just as the watch is the work of the watchmaker.

This comparison regards the universe as it does the watch, as a separate, independent and absolute entity. Nature is a thing in itself, complete and self-sufficient at this present moment. The only problem we face concerns not the existence but the cause of nature; not the present, but the past. Since in the eighteenth century the ultimate structure and order of nature were thought of in mechanical terms, its origin or creation was also conceived of as a mechanical process, comparable to the process of constructing a watch.

The shortcomings of this view lie in its taking both the watch and all of reality for granted. To our *radical amazement* [11] the ultimate problem is not only how it came into being, but also how is it that it is. The problem extends, furthermore, not only to the substance of the question, but to the act of asking the question as well. We are amazed at our ability to ask that question. We cannot take the existence of the watch as a safe starting point whose existence is given and which merely arouses the question of who brought it into being. *The watch itself is a mystery.*

There is no word in Biblical Hebrew for doubt; there are many words for wonder. Just as in dealing with judgments our starting-point is doubt, so in dealing with reality our starting-point is wonder. The Biblical man never questions the reality of the world around him. He never asks whether the rivers, mountains and stars are

73

only apparitions. His sense for the mind-surpassing grandeur of reality prevented the power of doubt from setting up its own independent dynasty. Doubt is an act in which the mind confronts its own ideas; wonder is an act in which the mind confronts the mystery of the universe. Radical scepticism is the outgrowth of conceit and subtle arrogance. Yet there was no conceit in the Prophets and no arrogance in the Psalmist.

And so the Biblical man never asks: Is there a God? To ask such a question, in which doubt is expressed as to which of two possible attitudes is true, means to accept the power and validity of a third attitude; namely the attitude of doubt. The Bible does not know doubt as an absolute attitude. For there is no doubt in which faith is not involved. The questions advanced in the Bible are of a different kind.

> Who has measured the waters in the hollow of his
>   hand,
> And marked off the heavens with a span,
> Enclosed the dust of the earth in a measure,
> And weighed the mountains in scales,
> And the hills in a balance?
>
> —Isaiah 40:12

This does not reflect a process of thinking that is neatly arranged in the order first of doubt, then faith; first the question, then the answer. It reflects a situation in which the mind stands *face to face* with the world rather than with its own ideas.

> Lift up your eyes and see!
> Who created these?
>
> —Isaiah 40:26

A question is an interrogative sentence calling for either a positive or a negative answer. But the sentence *Who created these?* is a question that contains the impossibility of one's giving a negative answer; it is an answer in disguise; *a question of amazement*, not of curiosity. This, then, is the prophet's thesis: There is a way of asking the great question which can only elicit an affirmative answer. What is the way?

> At the end of the days I, Nebuchadnezzar, lifted my eyes to heaven and my power of knowledge returned to me.

This confession, reported in the Book of Daniel (4:31), gives us an inkling of how one can recover one's power of knowledge: *to lift the eyes to heaven.* It is the same expression that Isaiah used: " Lift up your eyes on high and see: who created these? "

" What gives birth to religion is not intellectual curiosity, but the fact and experience of our being asked. . . . Faith is not the product of search and endeavor, but the answer to a challenge which no one can forever ignore." [12] The heaven is a challenge. When you lift up your eyes, you are faced with the question.

Lift up your eyes on high. There is a higher form of seeing. We must learn how to lift up our eyes on high in order to see that the world is more of a question than an answer.

In the spirit of Biblical tradition we must speak not of the foolishness of faith, but rather of *the foolishness of unbelief*, of *the scandal of indifference to God.* What is called in the English language an atheist, the language of the Bible calls *a fool.*[13] " The fool says in his heart, There is no God " (Psalms 14:1). The wicked is indifferent. In his pride " *he will not seek [after God]*: There is no God is the sum of his thoughts " (Psalms 10:4).

This attitude does not imply any easygoing rationalism,

the assumption, namely, that the belief in the God of Abraham, Isaac and Jacob is in complete agreement with the common habits and notions of the human mind. What it does mean is that the denial of Him is a scandal to the soul, to a soul in which the likeness of God is not distorted or misguided by false certainties. How it is possible not to believe? How is it possible not to sense the presence of God in the world? *" The lion has roared, who will not fear? "* (Amos 3:8).

There is a plane of living where no one can remain both callous and calm, unstunned and unabashed; where His presence may be defied but not denied, and where, at the end, faith in Him is the only way.[14]

The following parable was told by Rabbi Nahman of Bratslav:

> There was a prince who lived far away from his father, the king, and he was very, very homesick for his father. Once he received a letter from his father, and he was overjoyed and treasured it. Yet, the joy and the delight that the letter gave him increased his longing even more. He would sit and complain: " Oh, oh, if I could only touch his hand! If he would extend his hand to me, how I would embrace it. I would kiss every finger in my great longing for my father, my teacher, my light. Merciful father, how I would love to touch at least your little finger! " And while he was complaining, feeling and longing for a touch of his father, a thought flashed in his mind: Don't I have my father's letter, written in his own hand! Is not the handwriting of the king comparable to his hand? And a great joy burst forth in him.
>
> *When I look at the heavens, the work of Thy fingers.*
>
> —Psalms 8:4 [15]

76

CHAPTER FOUR

The Spiritual Crisis
and the
Social Predicament

A. POWELL DAVIES

Minister, All Souls Unitarian Church
Washington, D. C.

The Spiritual Crisis and
the Social Predicament

Our social predicament can be briefly stated: we are in danger of self-annihilation. We possess the means, or soon will possess them, of exterminating human society, and it is not clear what means we possess of averting this calamity.

As to how we reached this impasse, there is difference of opinion. There are those who look upon it as an organic process, essentially deterministic. Man being what he is, he was always certain to carry his knowledge and skill to the point of harnessing vast natural forces, and at the same time prove himself unequal to the human problem of wise guidance and restraint. There are others who believe that we are suffering the penalty of apostasy. We have given up believing doctrines and dogmas which it was sinful to disbelieve even though it seemed clear to us that they were not true. Hence, we must bear the penalty: it is the wrath of God.

There are still others, myself included, who reject both of these explanations and who think that, although the problem is far from simple, insights are available which can not only deepen understanding of our situation but also help us towards a mastery of it.

To continue for a moment, however, with some of the extreme views: Surely it is futile as well as erroneous to blame science and modern knowledge, as some are doing, for bringing the threat of catastrophe upon us. The human mind cannot set limits to its power of knowing; and knowledge, at any level, can be used for weal or woe. It is equally futile to blame ourselves for disbelieving what increasing knowledge had deprived of credibility. Nor is there any reason for supposing that if we had continued to believe these things, we would not now be in our present dangers.

There is indeed a spiritual crisis, and it is closely related to the social predicament. But in essence, it is less doctrinal than ethical. That is to say, it is not affected in important factors by the sanctions of particular doctrines: the apostasy was in believing that morality is not a part of human nature and that spiritual values are unreal.

" It is possible to go wrong in many ways, but right only in one." So declared Aristotle, in the fourth century, B. C., and until recent times, most of the world agreed with him. The modern age, however, to a greater extent than it has understood, forsook Aristotle and turned to Nietzsche. " It is absurd to speak of right and wrong *per se*," said Nietzsche. " Injury, violation, exploitation, annihilation, cannot be wrong in themselves, for life in its essence presupposes injury, violation, exploitation and annihilation." Or, in other words, far from there being many ways of going wrong and only one way of going right, right and wrong are just notions or conventions; they are rooted not in life itself, but only in prevailing misconceptions.

Largely persuaded of this, the modern world in due time produced a complete Nietzschean, a disciple who practiced precisely what his master had preached. His name was Hitler, and he almost succeeded in destroying civilization.

Awakened at last by the direness of the consequences of the Nietzschean view and aware of still further calamities which threaten to befall us, the modern world is now uncertain of itself and distrusts the Nietzschean principle. Could it be that Aristotle was correct? If so, what is his ground? What is it that we need to understand?

Conventional answers have been given to these questions, involving a return to traditional assumptions and submission to the ancient orthodoxies and authoritarian beliefs. But such answers are not deeply responsive to the questions asked. They are deficient in rationality and—except superficially—they are not persuasive. We must begin, I think, not with unproved and unprovable assumptions, but with life itself.

I shall therefore focus my own attention upon *the moral as natural*—or, to put it another way, upon the fact, as I believe it to be, that life at the human level is *naturally moral* and that it is this that we have failed to keep in view. I am well aware that there are other aspects of the problem, some of them important, but I believe that it is this one that should have the heaviest emphasis.

Let us begin our inquiry at a rather lowly—but realistic —level: All forms of life have patterns of behavior. They have them because they must. Without them, life itself could never have advanced beyond its first beginnings. Even a bacterium needs a pattern of behavior, one which enables it at the very least to absorb nourishment and to reproduce its species. If a bacterium deviates from this pattern (if, so to speak, it acts unbacterially), it invites its own destruction.

It is the same when we ascend in the scale of life to other levels, say the level of the insects. If an ant colony ceases to follow the behavior-pattern of an ant colony, it soon ceases to *be* an ant colony. It cannot survive except by following the behavior-pattern to which ants, by their very nature, are adapted. Moreover, fidelity to this pattern must be very largely spontaneous, or at least unforced from without. Each ant must want to act like an ant, and like an ant of a particular colony.

There are other forms of life, however, where this amount of regimentation is not necessary. Indeed, it would be fatal. Eagles must follow the behavior-patterns of eagles, not of ants. And so, every form of life from amoeba to zebra. Each follows its own behavior-pattern, but each *must have* a behavior-pattern to follow.

It is not otherwise when we come to man. Man is a form of life with a behavior-pattern which, at his level, includes conscious and voluntary choices between better and worse as tested by an end in view. It is not a rigid pattern in the sense that it never changes. It changes greatly in the evolution of man from the primitive to the civilized. It changes from one civilization to the next. But, nevertheless, it is always there; that is to say, there must always *be* a pattern, or human individuals become confused and society begins to drift toward disaster.

At the human level, this pattern cannot be instinctive. And although socially transmitted, it is not socially compulsive without the individual's assent. Man is different from the other animals. He can reason. Indeed, he *must reason.* He must reflect upon his own actions, and consider their consequences. He must deal selectively with his social inheritance, deciding whether he will follow existing patterns or establish new ones. Whatever he does—or fails to do—will leave him with a feeling of responsibility. His consciousness is not a mere extension of his animal awareness; it has a new dimension: the perception of values. If, in his relations with his fellow-man, he seeks his own advantage at the expense of others, he is inwardly condemned, and though he shut his ears he cannot escape this condemnation. Man is more free than other forms of life to choose his actions; but he is *not* free—not without disastrous consequences—to disregard his moral nature.

It is this that the Nietzscheans failed to understand. They thought that they could rebel against morality and still leave human nature essentially what it was—or even improved through "liberation." But it is impossible to rebel against morality without debasing, and, in the end, destroying human nature. To make man free " to injure, to violate, to exploit, to annihilate " is to make him less than human—to deprive him of the *human* in his nature.

The fact is not that morality is a voluntary adjunct to be accepted or rejected at pleasure: the fact is that *man is moral by nature. He cannot become amoral, non-moral, un-moral. He can only be moral or immoral.* This is not because he believes—or disbelieves—in supernatural sanctions or in any one particular religion. It is *because he is man* and cannot become anything less than man.

Let us see this fact a little more clearly. At the animal level, if patterns of behavior are confused, the animal life in question becomes depressed and loses its fitness to live. Many experiments have been made which prove this fact, such as the well-known experiments with rats. When the behavior-patterns of these animals have been sufficiently interfered with, they suffer the consequences of frustration and show symptoms of what in human beings we loosely call a " nervous breakdown." They develop, that is to say, the equivalent of a neurosis, or even of a psychosis, and after lingering for a while in increasing misery, they die. Or—for this also, apparently, is possible—the malady takes a more violent form and they become vicious in ways that never occur until their behavior-patterns are disturbed.

83

Well, how far away is this from what happens to a human society—and its human individuals—when the life of the society is similarly disturbed? Do we not see in our own society an ever-increasing incidence of the same sort of frustration malady? Why are there so many neurotics? Why so much recourse to psychiatrists? And why do whole nations fall victim to a sort of paranoia, as Germany did under Hitler and as we ourselves have recently shown signs of doing? Why are so many people ill at ease, reading every new book on peace of mind but never achieving peace of mind? How does it happen that we drift towards a world-engulfing disaster and are unable to assert ourselves sufficiently to change the course of events? Could it be that we are so far disintegrated as a human society, through the loss of our standards and the confusion of moral aims and purposes, that we are incapable of the behavior-pattern which could ensure survival? As we have seen, the behavior-pattern must be moral, for to be moral is our nature. If we reject morality, or sufficiently confuse it, we do not have a behavior-pattern which is sufficient for our purposes. And so, as individuals, we break down under the hopelessness and frustration of our individual lives; and as a society we decree our own destruction.

Let me remind you: In the case of the animal experiments we mentioned, the animals that are thrown into confusion become incapacitated for the effort to go on living, and after an interval of apathy, they die. In the case of human individuals and human societies, a similar condition is invited by an equivalent amount of frustration. And does anyone deny that this frustration exists? When people do not sufficiently believe in right and wrong, or have no standards which they are convinced

84

they are obliged to follow, they become confused. For
a brief interval, if the circumstances are favorable, they
may feel emancipated and exhilarated. They can do
"whatever they like." That is what they tell themselves.
But after a while, there is nothing that they *do* like.
Emotional fatigue sets in. They cannot make up their
minds. They become unable to choose. They remain
poised at a sort of dead center and can move neither one
way nor the other. It is in this condition that they come
to the psychiatrist or the minister or some other counselor;
or perhaps they persist so long that the final break is more
severe and they find themselves in an institution. Everything is then decided for them, and the hardest problem
of their rehabilitation is to get them to take charge of
their own lives once more.

Or there is another possibility, and in recent times,
we have seen it dramatically demonstrated. People with
no pattern for their lives, no basis of choice between good
and evil, no ethical standards which they accept as com-
pelling, may arrive at the condition I have just been
describing. But on the other hand, they may adopt such
standards as were set up by Hitler, or those offered by
the Kremlin. "You believe in nothing," said Hitler, in
the day of his triumph. "Why should you? There is
nothing to believe in. So you had better believe in me,
the man of power, the man of destiny! You can do this
easily because I do not believe in anything any more than
you do. I have no illusions. My contempt for you, you
can reproduce in *your* contempt for other people— particularly the people who think they are good people. You
can be *my* slaves and they shall be *your* slaves. And as
slaves you will not need to choose between good and evil.
You will not need to choose at all. You can obey. You

THE SPIRITUAL CRISIS AND THE SOCIAL PREDICAMENT

can be free from freedom! You can cast off the burden of liberty. See how your liberty frustrates you. See how it is driving you mad! Come to *me*. I will tell you from moment to moment what you must do. And you will not be *ordinary* slaves! You will be the most magnificent, most ferocious serfs and bondmen the world has ever known. Yes, listen to *me*! You are right in having no morality. Men *are* beasts of prey. In your case, instead of being the hunters, you are the hunted, the preyed upon —and by a lot of prating hypocrites. Come to me! Live life as it really is—brutally! "

That was Hitler's gospel—and it drew millions after him. The Kremlin message is less obviously barbarous. It is based, we are told, upon more civilized intentions. But it supplies the same relief to those who can no longer choose between right and wrong. The would-be idealist who has become morally confused is even more perverted by it than he would have been by Hitler. And much better than Hitler could have done, it provides a behavior-pattern, a design for living, a reprieve from frustration, a restored feeling of aim and purpose, which " saves " its devotees from spiritual dissolution.

Now, what it all portends—or so it seems to me—is either the disintegration of civilization, with perhaps a final, all-engulfing cataclysm, or a resurgence of civilized ethics —for how otherwise can we be saved? Perhaps there must be a revolution—a revolution *in* ethics—comparable in dynamic impact to the revolution *against* ethics of which the Nazi and Communist movements are the most positive manifestations. The Marxist philosophy, being materialist and determinist, is necessarily devoid of ethical founda-tions. I do not say it is devoid of ethical *content*, for it takes some of its content—inconsistently—from the civili-

zation it aims to destroy. But this content may be likened
to cut flowers, which, after a while must fade and die
because they are without roots and receive no nurture.
That is what has happened. That is why the early promise
of the Communist ideals, as Communists declared them,
has disappeared. You cannot maintain an ethical content
without ethical roots. And the Marxian materialism does
not permit of ethical roots. The nature of reality has
nothing to do with ethics—that is as much the Marxist
position as it was that of Nietzsche. And so it had to
follow, as the night the day, that whatever was ethically
good in Communism would be degraded into Sovietism—
would perish because it had no roots. This, then, was
part of the revolt—a clear consequence of the revolt—
against ethics, against morality, against right and wrong
as rooted in human nature and therefore in the nature
of reality.

And the answer to the present moral crisis must be a
reassertion of what Marx and Nietzsche—and their various
counterparts—denied. It must reassert that morality is a
natural, inescapable, and indestructible element in human
life, one that is neglected and resisted only at great cost
to human welfare, but which, if given appropriate nurture,
brings health and wholesomeness, sanity and security.

Not that any of this can come about through mere
revival of the dogmas of traditional religion. The age of
dogma—that sort of dogma—is over, and the effort to revive
it is essentially escapist. The new and more viable dogma
is the kind that Communism represents and it is this that
must be defeated. It cannot be defeated by attempting to
resuscitate discredited beliefs, or by expecting God to do
what He will never do—intervene to save us. This can
only increase our frustration, for we shall never really

THE SPIRITUAL CRISIS AND THE SOCIAL PREDICAMENT

believe what the age of science has rendered unbelievable. Nor can we, without mortal loss, surrender the moral nature that God has given us and ask to be changed into spiritual puppets. What we need is a resurgence of civilized ethics and this can only be achieved by opening the door to natural religion, and by understanding that human morality is discovered and corroborated, not through the sanctions of dogmatic affirmations, but *empirically*, in what reveals itself in human nature and in history.

This does not mean that we shall leave out of account the great religious teachers of ancient times; on the contrary, we shall know that these teachers, like ourselves, are ethical revolutionaries. They, like us, do not place their reliance in the provincialisms of special and particular beliefs, even when they entertain these beliefs—or when, for themselves, they accept them. They look, as we must, for the universal.

And it is their testimony, as it is our own increasing insight, that it is at the level of the moral that man fulfills himself or is defeated. Though he gain the whole world of knowledge and power, if he loses what religion calls his soul, knowledge and power will not avail him—indeed, they will destroy him, even as they are threatening to do at the present time. If man betrays the truth—the difficult, inward truth, that only an honest and persistent intention can search out—he betrays his humanity also; if he descends from intellect to cunning, and from morality to opportunism, he will not succeed in merely lowering himself to the level of the beasts of the field; he will fall lower. For what in them is natural, in him is deformity. If he turns away from justice, injustice decrees his dissolution. The moral and the spiritual are not optional, mere ornaments of life; they are essential, mandatory, the very essence of our human nature divested of which* life has nothing left but degradation and corruption.

For man *as* man, there is fulfillment. For man as anything less, there is only annihilation. That is the fact about man—the fact of his nature *as* man—which cannot be ignored, repudiated, or expunged. The measure of man must be his moral measure; anything less becomes the scope of his calamity. And this is true, not in one place, or because revealed religion has declared it: It is true in all places and because *reality* declares it.

Its verification is in history and its long sequence of tragedies. It is corroborated by the decline and fall of every civilization that has ever lived and died upon the earth. It is plain in every individual human life that has opposed it. Truth, justice, sympathy, benevolence, gentleness—these and all the other virtues are written not upon stone in codes and commandments, but in flesh and blood. Brotherhood—it is not a thing to which we may come because we are exhorted: we *are* brothers. The oneness of the human family is required by the nature of human society itself. To reject brotherhood is to reject life—and quite literally, for a world that refuses the brotherhood of man is a world which consents to die and which will bring upon itself its own destruction.

These things are true, true not as assertion or opinion, but true as the earth and sky are true, true with their own truth and needing no other to support them. And that is why there must be an ethical resurgence. Some of what it brings may be new—new in pattern, perhaps, but in any case, new in clarity and emphasis. But mostly, it will be neither new nor old, but a restored and intensified recognition of what man really *is*, and of what reality— and some of us would say, reality's God—expects of him.

Where the ethical resurgence comes, human life will reach new levels. It will have meaning and direction to an extent unknown at present. And in a way understood and made manifest only by the exemplars and the truly great teachers of religion, human life will be religious. Man will know and declare that no matter what the mystery of his being, he is and must be, by his very nature, a living soul. He will meet his God, not in his creeds, but in the freedom of his honest thought—and in the yearnings of his heart for goodness.

When we accept fully our moral nature and what it implies in social responsibility, when we see how it has grown and developed and the universal scope of what it now asks of us, when we recognize the justice of its claim, we shall have a new premise for our program for the world. We cannot ensure even our own survival on the basis of our present premises. Week by week, we move nearer to the abyss. Our military provisions are necessities, but they do not turn away the threat. Our power to destroy is the measure of our own destruction. What we can do to others, others can do to us.

We need a wider program, and this we can have only on the basis of the fullest recognition of our moral nature. It must be a program that accepts the claim of all mankind upon us. The retarded multitudes who are no longer fatalistic about their destitution but have seen the promise of a better life justly demand our help. The future will be decided—unless annihilistic war decides it—by what these people do, by the way of life they adopt. *We* cannot survive except by their consent—except through their cooperation. But we have resisted their demand upon us. We have exploited them on the Nietzschean basis instead of accepting them as brothers, entitled to share the common effort and the common recompense. And we have done this because we have ignored—indeed, at times have tried to expel—our moral nature.

Yet, the truth is plain. We have failed as we were bound to fail, and now we are threatened with destruction. Our human predicament is the result of our moral abdication. Nothing can save us but a new insurgence of morality —perhaps it should be called an ethical revolution.

And what is true of the world without is true of the life within. There will be no rest—no rest for the mind of man, here or anywhere—until this ethical revolution is begun. When it *is* begun, and I hope I may say " when " and not " if," we shall know as it was never known before that human life fulfills itself not in the dissipation of its substance for the brief and feverish joy of living out its moment in a world of anarchy and moral mutiny—and after that, the emptiness and void; but in rising to the fullness of its stature, God-like, breathing yet more deeply the immortal breath that breathed itself into the dust of earth at the beginning, when the word was spoken—" and man became a living soul! "

That is what we must learn—must learn it as it was never learned before. And if we will permit it, this violent, tempestuous time may yet become our teacher, revealing to us the truth of our own nature, the reality of good and evil and the choice we make between them, while God waits for his children, made in his own image, to bear at last his likeness, soul unto soul.

CHAPTER FIVE

Religion and Theology in a Theory of the Cultural Sciences

HAROLD A. BASILIUS

Professor of German
Wayne University

Religion and Theology in a Theory
of the Cultural Sciences

Lo you now, how vainly mortal men do blame the
gods! For of us they say comes evil, whereas they even
of themselves, through the blindness of their own
hearts, have sorrows beyond that which is ordained.
—ODYSSEY, I, 35 ff.

B ASIC TO THE development of my thesis, indeed to
the development of any thesis, is a clarification and definition of the basic terms. I am using three of them: religion,
theology, and the cultural sciences.

An inclusive definition of the term *religion* might
indeed be very difficult. It has frequently been stated that
this is the case, and only as recently as 1951 in our country
a very elaborate statement and development of the idea
was made by Henry Alden Bunker [1] and slightly earlier
in 1947 by Edward Hitschman.[2] By using the technique
of liberal and extended quotation both authors show
clearly the continuing and universal attraction of the
fundamental problem which religion presents as well as
the inherent complexity of the problem.

I personally understand by the term *religion* all those
cultural manifestations, and they are indeed many,
throughout all areas of the humanities and the social
sciences, that result from the human feeling of cosmic
awe. The human feeling of minuteness, unrelatedness,
and even fear, as he stands before and contemplates the

95

enormity which is the universe, has caused man to seek support and comfort in revelation and in ritual and in his god; and his culture has created buildings, manuscripts, oral and written poetry, sculpture, painting, social institutions, charters, church organizations, creeds, customs, value codes, and a hundred other forms which give expression to this feeling of awe before the great cosmos.

As I use the term, then, religion has reference to an attitude, a state of mind, a stance. It is a psychological phenomenon in the first place, and to a lesser extent a philosophical or historical or sociological one. There is little if anything rational about it. Rationality enters only into the examination of the phenomenon. Rationality has to do, then, with theology or whatever other disciplines are concerned with the rational or scientific investigation of the cultural phenomena which result from the religious feeling of cosmic awe. This is essentially the same distinction which Paul Tillich makes in his lecture between essentialist and existentialist analyses and problems.

The distinction is neatly brought out by Friedrich Nietzsche in a letter to his sister: " Here the ways of men part: if you wish to strive for peace of soul and pleasure, then believe; if you wish to be a devotee of truth, then inquire." [3] The former refers to religion, the latter to theology.

My allusion to Nietzsche is obviously from a context altogether different from the commonly current one in our country, the context which is exemplified by Dr. Powell Davies elsewhere in this volume. Dr. Davies projects a notion of Nietzsche as being exclusively the precursor of Adolf Hitler. That is, to be sure, an aspect of Nietzsche, but not at all in the sense that Nietzsche's thinking anticipated or hoped to bring into being the monstrosity which was Hitler. As a matter of fact, Nietzsche would have been the first exile from Hitler's Germany, had he been living. The propensity of American culture to fix on this one, in my judgment, this lesser, aspect of Nietzsche is owing in part to the bias of our culture, but perhaps in greater part to unfortunate books about Nietzsche such as that of Professor Crane Brinton. Although this disapproving interpretation of Nietzsche was abetted somewhat by the disillusionment of the German diaspora which settled in America, for example, Henrich Mann; and, understandably so; all Germans including those of the diaspora are aware of the other and more important facets of Nietzsche. I personally value Nietzsche very highly and quote from him lovingly and with respect.

But listen now, if you please, to a selection of opinions regarding what religion is and of what it consists, opinions of various important people who have contributed to the truly gigantic literature on this subject:

> Accepting it then as axiomatic that a definition, while it may indeed contain the truth, can hardly include the whole truth, we may look without condescension upon such a pronouncement as Matthew Arnold's, who defined religion, more aphoristically than precisely, as "morality tinged with emotion"— or on Max Müller's, who, with a sweepingness which would seem to embrace rather more than the thing defined, said that "any thing that lifts man above the realities of this material life is religion"; nor did he greatly improve upon this in stating on another occasion that "religion consists in the perception of the infinite under such manifestations as are able to influence the moral character of man." To Herbert Spencer the essence and kernel of all religions was on the one hand the sense of mystery, but on the other

RELIGION AND THEOLOGY AS CULTURAL SCIENCES

an instinctive desire and demand to penetrate this
mystery—representing thus, above all, man's desire to
know the unknown, the unknowable. Religion is defined by [Emile] Durkheim, if chiefly from the stand-
point of observance and ritual, as the [" ensemble of
practises which are concerned with sacred matters "]—
and of the word " sacred," with its double meaning
of " holy " and " accursed," it has been said (by E. E.
Crawley) that " no other term covers the whole of
religious phenomena and a survey of the complex
details of various worships results in showing that
no other conception will cover the whole body of
religious facts." To the definitions of religion already
noted might be added, among the many others, Cardi-
nal Newman's, " The essence of religion is authority
and obedience," Schleiermacher's designation of religion as a " feeling of absolute dependence," and
[Marie Jean] Guyau's description of the " religious
sense " as " the sense of dependence in relation to wills
which primitive man places in the universe." Such
conceptions are somewhat enlarged upon in the definition of religion proposed by Sir James Frazer: " A
propitiation or conciliation of powers superior to
men which are believed to control the course of
human life "; or, laying more emphasis upon a state
of mind than upon the acts of propitiation and
conciliation induced or impelled thereby, there is
Howerth's, " Religion is the effective desire to be in
the right relation to the Power manifesting itself
in the universe." Certainly there must here be included, too, Tylor's famous " minimum definition "
of religion as " the belief in spiritual beings "—
that is to say, " spirits " in the wide sense that includes
" souls," a definition which R. R. Marett has supple-
mented—because of his surely well-founded opinion
that primitive rudimentary religion is at once a wider

and in certain respects a vaguer thing than " the belief
in spiritual beings "—by including therein " much of
what hitherto has been classed as magic," terming
" pre-animistic " this so-called " magical " element
and the type of religion in which it prevails (as
though, in point of fact, it did not prevail in every
religion, or, more precisely, loom large in every religious practice). I would conclude this paragraph
with the assertion of Leuba that " [religion] is the
Agent or the Power with which man thinks himself
in relation, and through whom he endeavors to secure
the gratification of his desires, which alone is distinc-
tive of religious life, and so the idea of the origin of
gods, though not identical with the origin of religion,
is at any rate its central problem." Wherewith we
may bring to an end this fairly representative if
nevertheless quite random selection of opinions regarding what religion is and of what it consists; adding
only Statius' assertion about the " origin of gods " . . .
(*primus in orbe deos fecit timor*) —with its echo, if
you like, in Hobbes's, " The feare of things invisible
is the natural seed of religion." It is inescapable, in
sum, that fear on the one hand, and a sense of
dependence, on the other, form the warp and woof
of religion as defined by those who have been cited.[4]

At the end of the passage which I just quoted, Mr.
Bunker has an interesting linguistic observation in the
form of a note. In it he points out that the etymology
of the word *religion* is obscure. Some people, beginning
with Cicero, want to relate the word to the Latin *religere*,
which is the antithesis of *negligere*, and thus have it mean,
in short, a vigilant care, a pious observance, as opposed to
indifference and negligence. A more recent view wants to
relate the word to the Latin *religare*, which means to

hold back, bind fast. Religion would in that derivation mean taboo or restraint. This brings to mind the observation of Sigmund Freud, corroborated by many linguists, that words basic to a culture frequently combine antithetical meanings, for example, the Greek *hagios* (whence our *hagiology*) the Latin *sacer* and the French *sacré* all signify both sacred and holy on the one hand and accursed or damned on the other. Both of the antithetical meanings have in common, of course, the idea of the forbidden, the not-to-be-spoken, the not-to-be-touched, the not-to-be-entered.[5]

William James in his book *The Varieties of Religious Experience*, which, as you know, is the American classic on this subject, explicitly points to the ambivalence of the term *religion* in the following words: " Does God really exist? How does He exist? What is He? [These] are so many irrelevant questions. Not God, but life, more life, a larger, richer, more satisfying life, is, in the last analysis, the end of religion." But in another place in the book he says: " The warring gods and formulae of the various religions do indeed cancel each other, but there is a certain uniform deliverance in which religions all appear to meet. It consists of two parts: an uneasiness, and its solution. The solution is a sense that we are saved from the wrongness, from the sense that there is something wrong about us." [6]

It is well-known that Sigmund Freud devoted a great deal of attention to the problem of religion and wrote very discerningly about it. This preoccupation of psychoanalysis with religion has to my mind a special significance, for it illustrates the diversity of aspects in which religious phenomena can and must be studied.[7] In a very persuasive essay, perhaps one of the most persuasive he ever wrote,

entitled "The Future of an Illusion," Freud, speaking
of the many religious ideas which have exercised so strong
an influence on mankind, says that the ideas are "born
from the need to make tolerable the helplessness of his
own childhood and the childhood of the human race."
Freud believes that religious ideas have sprung from the
same need as have all other cultural achievements: namely,
the necessity for defending ourselves against the crushing
supremacy of nature with its elements which seem to
mock at all human control, such as earthquake, whirlwind,
flood, diseases, and, above all, the painful and insoluble
riddle of death, forces which "bring again to mind our
weakness and helplessness, of which we thought the work
of civilization had rid us." The real reason-for-being of
culture and its chief task is, then, according to Freud, " to
defend us against nature." [8] Henri Bergson reached a
comparable conclusion in his book *The Two Sources of
Morality and Religion* (1932).

By way of concluding this definition of religion and
thereby returning also to my own original definition that
religion was or had reference to the cultural manifestations
resulting from the human feeling of cosmic awe, let me
quote a very revealing passage from the essay by Edward
Hitschmann:

> We cannot avoid the conclusion that in religion
> we have a department of human nature with un-
> usually close relation to the transmarginal or sub-
> liminal region. If the word " subliminal " is offensive
> to any of you, as smelling too much of psychical
> research or other aberrations, call it by any name
> you please, to distinguish it from the level of full
> sunlit consciousness. Call this latter the A region of
> personality, if you care to, and call the other the B

region. The B region is then obviously the larger part of each of us, for it is the abode of everything that is latent and the reservoir that passes unrecorded or unobserved. It contains, for example, such things as all our momentarily inactive memories and it harbors the springs of all our obscurely motivated passions, impulses, likes, dislikes and prejudices. Our intuitions, hypotheses, fancies, superstitions, persuasions, convictions and in general all our non-rational operations, come from it. It is the source of our dreams, and apparently they may return to it. In it arise whatever mystical experiences we may have and our automatisms, sensory or motor; our life in hypnotic and " hypoid " conditions, if we are subject to such conditions; our delusions, fixed ideas and hysterical accidents, if we are hysteric subjects; our supranormal cognitions, if there be any, and if we are telepathic subjects. It is also the fountainhead of much that feeds our religion. In persons deep in the religious life, we have now abundantly seen—and this is my conclusion—the door into this region seems unusually wide open; at any rate, experiences making their entrance through that door have had emphatic influence in shaping religious history." [9]

Professor T. V. Smith concludes that Ralph Barton Perry in his *Realms of Values* conceives of religion as that " which men would acquire if they were to start again, deprived of every inherited religious establishment," [10] and this, Professor Smith thinks, is a very tough-minded formulation of the problem.

In the series of quotations which I have just offered, I have actually anticipated a definition of my second term, namely, *theology*. I have already indicated that theology is rational and by that token a science in the more traditional sense of that term. It is an intellectual discipline whose purpose is the ordering of the lore of God, to play on the etymological meaning of the term. Significant in this connection is the observation of William James that out of theology a new science would and ought to develop, namely, the science of religions. " If philosophy will abandon metaphysics and deduction for criticism and induction," he says, "she can make herself enormously useful, frankly transforming herself from theology into a science of religions. Why should a critical science of religions not eventually command as general a public adhesion as is commanded by a physical science! Even the personally non-religious might accept its conclusions on trust." [11]

In a similar vein the renowned Biblical scholar Robert Casey declared that "there is a great need for new material of a kind more susceptible for experimental observation and control. . . . The psychological evaluation of religion in terms of evidence rather than hypothesis would represent a substantial gain." [12]

The anthropologist Clyde Kluckhohn makes the challenging observation that whereas prior to the nineteenth century theology was a science derived from philosophy, after the nineteenth century the science of cultural anthropology has derived from religion. Kluckhohn goes on to develop the notion that whereas in medieval philosophy, philosophy itself was regarded as the *scientia scientiarum*, the queen of the sciences, the new discipline of cultural anthropology is and properly should become the new queen in our day.[13]

Whether one refer to the discipline as being theology or a science of religions or cultural anthropology, there is a growing consensus that values and value-schemes are

103

RELIGION AND THEOLOGY AS CULTURAL SCIENCES

basic to the structure and function of cultures. Theologians and anthropologists agree on this. An exciting vista of new scholarship suggests itself in which the older and more established kind of investigation joins hands with the ¹new in re-examining cultural phenomena such as language, custom, ritual, the arts, etc., from the point of view of studying them as expressions of values and value patterns, all of which imply a metaphysic of one kind or another.¹⁴

Theology, then, like all other disciplines or sciences, is an aspect of culture. The sciences do not stand outside culture but are an integral part of it. Hence, despite a certain common logic and method, there are as many kinds of science as there are cultures: hence, there are also varieties of theologies, which range from Thomism, which is the rational ordering of God-lore in the etymological sense of the word *theology*, to the more personal, idiosyncratic, and ideological theologies of some so-called liberal theologians which, to be sure, seem to many to be neither liberal nor theological.

Among contemporary Protestant theologians, for example, the diversity of thought between Albert Schweitzer, Paul Tillich, and Reinhold Niebuhr on the one hand and the Fundamentalists on the other is truly amazing. Niebuhr points up this diversity in a recent review of Canon Charles E. Raven's *Natural Religion and Christian Theology* (Cambridge, 1953) in the following well-nigh irreconcilable terms:

> His [Raven's] lectures make a competent survey of what classical mysticism and Christianity have in common and to what degree the witness of metaphysical speculations agrees with the truth as apprehended by Christian faith. It is not evident that he

104

fully understands the crucial issue between Christianity in its classical form and that part of the Christian movement known as " liberal " Christianity, and which is characterized by its effort to adjust Christian truth to the achievements and also (unfortunately) to the illusions of our culture. That issue is whether human freedom is subject to indeterminate possibilities of good and evil (as Biblical faith insists) or whether the growth of human freedom guarantees the gradual moral perfection of man. This proposition is at the basis of every form of liberalism whether religious or secular.[15]

Niebuhr thus identifies a basic theological problem with a general cultural one, which recalls the observation of Karl Marx to the effect that " it is not the consciousness of men that determines their existence, but on the contrary their social existence determines their consciousness." [16]

To further exemplify the contemporary inclination to identify basic theological problems with general cultural ones, I should like to cite two statements, the first of them by the eminent Catholic sociologist, Dr. John Courtney Murray of Woodstock College. The piece in point is a lecture, which he delivered in 1949 in New York under the title " The Natural Law." I have chosen this particular lecture by Father Murray, first, because it distinctly states the notion that we in our time face a series of possible choices requiring vigorous intellectual debate and all the resources of our scholarship before we can be completely clear about the merits of the basic issues which are involved. Second, this lecture is particularly provocative because it represents the effort of an extremely learned Catholic to show that, from his point of view, everything which we understand by the term *natural law* is not the product of eighteenth and nineteenth century, essentially anti-Catholic, thinking, but is on the contrary a very essential and very old component of traditional Catholic philosophy. The context from which I quote involves two main points: 1) the age in which we are living is an age that seeks order; 2) order must presuppose a metaphysic, that is, some principle of the good, of justice, of right, which is absolute and outside of experience; otherwise, as you will hear Father Murray say, " we are writing on sand in a time of hurricanes and floods."

First in importance is the metaphysical character of natural law, its secure anchorage in the order of essences—the ultimate order of beings and purposes. As a metaphysical idea, the idea of natural law is timeless, and for that reason timely; for what is timeless is always timely. But it has an added timeliness. An age of order is by definition a time for metaphysical decisions. They are being made all round us; and no one escapes making them; one merely escapes making this one rather than that one. *Our* decisions, unlike those of the eighteenth century, cannot be purely political, because our reflection on the bases of society and the problem of its freedom and its order must be much more profound. And this in turn is so because these problems stand revealed to us in their depths; one cannot any longer, like John Locke, be superficial about them. Our reflection, therefore, on the problem of freedom and of human rights must inevitably carry us to a metaphysical decision in regard of the nature of man. Just as we now know that the written letter of a Bill of Rights is of little value unless there exist the institutional means whereby these rights may have, and be guaranteed, their expression in social action, so

also we know—or ought to know—that it is not enough
for us to be able to concoct the written letter unless
we are likewise able to justify, in terms of ultimates
in our own thinking about the nature of man, our
assertion that the rights we list are indeed rights and
therefore inviolable, and human rights and therefore
inalienable. Otherwise we are writing on sand in a
time of hurricanes and floods.

There are perhaps four such ultimate decisions
open to our making, and each carries with it the
acceptance of certain political consequences. First,
one could elect to abide by the old Liberal individual-
ism. At bottom then one would be saying that
" natural rights " are simply individual material interests (be they of individuals or social groups or nations),
so furnished with an armature by positive law as to
be enforceable by the power of government. In this
view one would be consenting to a basically atomist
concept of society, to its organization in terms of
power relationships, to a concept of the state as simply
an apparatus of compulsion without the moral function of realizing an order of justice; for in this view
there is no order of justice antecedent to positive law
or contractual agreements. In a word, one would be
accepting today's national and international *status
quo*; for one would be accepting its principles.

Secondly, by an extreme reaction to individualistic
Liberalism, wherein the individual as an individual
is the sole bearer of " rights," one could choose the
Marxist concept of " human rights " as based solely
on social function, economic productivity. One would
then be saying that all " rights " are vested in the state,
which is the sole determinant of social function; it
is the state that is free, and the individual is called
simply to share its freedom by pursuing its purposes,

107

which are determined by the laws of dialectical materialism. In this view one would be consenting to the complete socialization of man (his mind and will, as well as his work), within the totalitarian state, all his energies being requisitioned for the realization of a pseudo-order of " justice," which is the triumph of collective man over nature in a classless society that will know no " exploitation of man by man." In this view, as in the foregoing one, one accepts as the ultimate reality the material fact of power—in one case the power of the individual, in the other the power of the collectivity. One bases society and the state on a metaphysic of force (if the phrase be not contradictory).

A third decision, that somehow attempts a mediation between these extreme views, is soliciting adherents today; I mean the theory that its protagonists call " modern evolutionary scientific humanism," but that *I* shall call " the new rationalism." It is a rationalism, because its premise is the autonomy of man, who transcends the rest of nature and is transcended by nothing and nobody (at least nothing and nobody knowable). It is new, because (unlike the old rationalism) it maintains (with Spinoza, whom Bowle has pointed to as one of its earliest forerunners) that " man " is something more than " reason." It identifies " natural law " (though the term is not frequent with it) with " the drive of the whole personality," the totality of the impulses whereby men strive to " live ever more fully." It is new, too, because it abandons the old rationalist passion for deductive argument and for the construction of total patterns in favor of the new passion for scientific method and the casting up of provisional and partial hypotheses. Finally, it is new because it does not, like eighteenth

century rationalism, conceive " nature " and its laws,
or the " rights of man," as static, given once for all,
needing only to be " discovered." It adds to the old
rationalistic universe the category of time; it supple-
ments the processes of reason with the processes of
history and the consequent experience of change and
evolution. . . .

These then are three possible metaphysical decisions
that one can make as a prelude to the construction of
the age of order; none of them, I think, carries a
promise that the age will truly *be* one of order. There
remains the fourth possible decision—the option of
natural law in the old traditional sense. Here the
decision is genuinely metaphysical; one does not opt
for a rationalization of power, but for a metaphysic
of right. I say " right " advisedly, not " rights "; the
natural law does not in the first instance furnish a
philosophy of human rights in the sense of subjective
immunities and powers to demand; this philosophy is
consequent on the initial furnishing of a philosophy
of right, of justice, of law, of a juridical order, and
of social order. The reason is that natural law thinking does not set out, as Locke did, from the abstract,
isolated individual, and ask what are his " inalienable
rights " as an individual. Rather, it regards the community as " given " equally with the person; man is
regarded as a member of an order constituted by
God, and subject to the laws that make the order an
order—laws that derive from the nature of man, which
is as essentially social as it is individual. In the natural
law climate of opinion (very different from that set
by the " law of nature "), objective law has the
primacy over subjective rights; law is not simply the
protection of rights but their source, because it is
the foundation of duties.[17]

From a diametrically opposite point of view, A. Powell Davies also identifies a theological problem with a cultural one. Mr. Davies is discussing another recent book by Canon Charles E. Raven, entitled *Science and Religion* (Cambridge, 1952), and writes as follows:

> The first consequence, therefore, of the ascendancy of science was open conflict with the churches. It was rather pitiful that this should have been chiefly dramatized by the " Geology versus *Genesis* " debate, for the questions at issue were much wider. But in any case, as Dr. Raven emphasizes, although the churches tried to make out the wrong case, there was a right case which they should certainly have argued. The scientists had taken a very narrow position which later events were to prove untenable; and in taking it, they [gave] considerable impetus not only to Karl Marx who made it the basis of his political theories, but also to capitalist imperialism which justifies its ruthless competition and its exploitation by appeal to what was looked upon as scientific realism.

> This was the early impact of modern science. It was succeeded by a period of uneasy truce. The scientific method was demonstrating its validity, not only theoretically but in spectacular technological results. The churchmen had to make concessions. This produced on the one hand the near-abandonment of theology and the spread of humanism, and on the other, the erection of boundaries between the fields of science and religion, making possible the new orthodoxies.

> Meanwhile, the true ground of reconciliation was neither humanism, which surrendered too much territory to agnosticism, nor the neo-orthodoxy, which,

in spite of its negative merits, produced chiefly intellectual folklore. The true ground was naturalism, which after the drastic revisions of scientific assumptions associated with such names as Einstein and Planck, offered genuine opportunities for an integrated religio-scientific outlook.

This, unfortunately, is far too little understood. Canon Raven himself is not willing to abandon the supernatural as a convenient category though he does in fact place it clearly within the realm of nature. But at least he is not misleading. Unlike some other writers, he knows that the famous Einstein formula $e = mc^2$ is not a corroboration of St. Paul's Epistle to the Romans and that the quantum theory is not an endorsement of the Apostles' Creed. Whatever theologians may wish to argue on other grounds than those of scientific findings—and it is necessary that they should—science itself can go no further than natural religion. Even this is not to say that science affirms religious principles; but it does today offer no opposition to belief in the moral and spiritual values as rooted in ultimate reality. Individual scientists, speaking as entire persons and not relying merely upon scientific theory, may well go further than this and affirm that what they have learned under severe intellectual discipline has encouraged their religious faith. But it is well to regard these affirmations as those of the individuals themselves and to remind ourselves that although the scientific method should be applied as widely as possible, the truth remains that life is larger than science and the human quest is a many-sided one.[18]

Any discussion of the integral relation to its culture of theology or the science of religions or cultural anthropology would, I feel, be incomplete at this time if mention were not made of a particularly able and lucid philosophical analysis contributed recently by Harold Taylor, president of Sarah Lawrence College. The analysis is in the form of an essay about which I have been talking enthusiastically to my colleagues and friends for the past two years. Many of my colleagues and friends are very disdainful of anything Harold Taylor says simply because he is an educational functionalist. That is Taylor's own term for what is more vulgarly known as a progressive educationist. Unfortunately, it doesn't help much when I point out that even though he is a progressivist, Harold Taylor is thoroughly trained in philosophy. My friends simply refuse to believe this, or if they do believe it, they regard Taylor as just another good philosopher gone wrong. They used to feel that way about John Dewey, too, but this point of view has changed somewhat since Dewey has been canonized.

Taylor is not talking in his essay specifically about the relation of theology to culture. He is, as a matter of fact, discussing educational philosophy with particular reference to the higher learning. In discussing the role of the humanities in higher education, he divides all philosophy, as Caesar did all of Gaul, into three groups. Two of them are radical and extreme. The third represents a middle-of-the-road position and is representative of perhaps as many as ninety percent of practicing humanists. (I use this term for want of a briefer one merely to designate teacher-scholars operating in the humanities and not as a taboo word to imply something intrinsically superior.) The radical extremes are what Taylor calls on the one hand the absolutists or rationalists and on the other hand the functionalists or pragmatists or instrumentalists. He points out that the keystone disciplines of the absolutists are metaphysics and philosophy and their chief emphasis, the intellect. Father Murray would illustrate this extreme. Educationally, St. John's College would serve the same purpose. The keystone disciplines of the functionalists are psychology in combination with aesthetics. The functionalists are concerned with understanding problems of human development and human expression. Sarah Lawrence College or Bennington College would illustrate this point of view in their educational practice. The absolutists are obviously rigid with respect to their premises as well as to the logical consequences developed from these. The functionalists, on the other hand, are flexible, tentative, experimental, tolerant. They eagerly anticipate the future and its developments, whereas the absolutists tend to emphasize the importance of the tradition and of the fact that there are no contemporary problems the answers to which have not been adequately anticipated by the philosophy of the Western tradition. From the point of view of the absolutists there exists what Aldous Huxley likes to call the perennial philosophy (*philosophia perennis*). The functionalists believe that given time to learn a little more about the psychological structure and functioning of human beings and to develop the aesthetic and creative potential of human beings, we will have made a tolerable start on the road to developing an adequate philosophy of life.

In contrast to these two extremes, a middle-of-the-road position, which Taylor calls the eclectic or neo-humanist position and which represents the point of view of the vast majority of practicing humanists, concentrates on history as its keystone discipline. It therefore inclines also to emphasize the past and the primacy of the intellect in common with the absolutists. The neo-humanists believe that the present and its problems can be clarified only by understanding the past. The basic assumption of the neo-humanists is the belief or the hope that a knowledge of the good, as this may be learned from history, will bring a commitment to the good. They come close in this respect to the problem of liberal Protestant theology, alluded to by Reinhold Niebuhr: namely, faith in the gradual and ultimate perfectibility of human material. Like the functionalists, the neo-humanists are, in general, tolerant, but they are also distrustful of the newer learning. The very term *science* generally makes them unhappy, and they incline to regard the psychology of personal development as a rather shoddy pseudo-discipline invented by colleges of education in collusion with the devil. Social action, which is a prime purpose of the functionalists, is regarded by the neo-humanists as essentially unacademic, lacking in academic dignity and violating that part of the academic canon which allegedly accords the scholar the right to pursue truth in isolation from the community of daily living. In brief, the neo-humanists, though tolerant, are skeptical and individualistic. Their position is essentially negative rather than positive with respect to the practical solution of human problems, either personal or social.

Harold Taylor's treatment of the subject is another illustration for me of that summary and interpretative kind of scholarship which I think our time needs so desperately and which the cultural sciences can provide. His thumbnail sketch of the three essential philosophical positions emphasizes attitudes, inclinations, stances, and only incidentally subject-matter. Like Father Murray, Taylor presents philosophy in terms of alternatives between which human beings must make choices. In relating the choices to various disciplines, however, Taylor contributes substantially to the theory or to *a* theory of the cultural sciences and highlights the essential importance of greater cooperation, of increased mutual trust and confidence, and finally of sympathetic understanding among the academic disciplines. When Joseph Conrad in his preface to *The Nigger of the Narcissus* insisted upon the underlying unity of aim which is shared by the artist, the thinker, and the scientist, all three being intent solely upon arriving at the truth, he was also stating an ideal for the scholar and for the community of scholars which is a university, which is too frequently lost sight of but which, particularly in our time, has become a crucial necessity.[19]

In thus coming gradually to the third term of my title: namely, the cultural sciences, I have been deliberately implying from the beginning that I regard all cultural phenomena (including theology but particularly also religion) as capable of scientific study. To study anything at all, including religion and theology, means to deal with them scientifically in that original sense of science as cognitive knowledge. I use the term *science*, then, as meaning organized common sense, as Thomas Henry Huxley defined it, or as being " simply organized knowledge " in the words of Professor George Sarton.[20] I never mean by science what my former teacher, the late Professor Leonard Bloomfield, together with others liked to call physicalism: that is, a mode of operation based on the assumption that all phenomena can be atomized into quantifiable physical data and, indeed, that phenomena which cannot be thus atomized are not capable of being dealt with scientifically.

My title intends to imply that all of the disciplines that we now subsume under the social sciences and the humanities together constitute the cultural sciences.

It should be clear from this that I emphatically reject

115

the notion that either the humanities exclusively or the social sciences exclusively, as Stuart Chase, for example, would suggest, constitute the cultural sciences. The unfortunate situation in which the humanities and the social sciences feel themselves to be in opposition to each other is doubtless to be explained by the relatively recent origin of the social sciences and also by the unfortunate connotations that attach themselves to the taboo word *science*. The complementary usefulness of the anthropologist-sociologist on the one hand and of the humanist on the other is now so abundantly clear as hardly to need further discussion. It is rather well-known, for example, how greatly aesthetic theory has in the past twenty-five years been powerfully affected by the results of anthropological researches dealing with primitive painting, sculpture, music, and poetry. Conversely, anthropologists have been so greatly impressed by the work in American linguistics during the past quarter of a century that Indiana University two years ago established a conference for the mutual discussion by linguists and anthropologists of their methods and results relative to the problem of human language. And last year at the same university there was a similar conference between linguists and psychologists, following an earlier conference between them at Cornell in 1951. In brief, then, American scholarship can no longer afford to isolate the social sciences and the humanities from each other. Their specialized kinds of knowledge obviously all bear on the same human problem and are mutually indispensable to each other's successful work.

It seems to me ludicrous that my colleagues in the social sciences and in the humanities find it necessary so frequently to defend their work on the grounds that it, too, is scientific in the same measure that research in physics,

chemistry, geology, etc., is scientific. It is so utterly obvious
that the work of the social scientist and the humanist are
as scientific as is the work of the physical scientist that
constant reiteration of the fact acquires a quality of the
pathetic that suggests whistling in the dark. Disparity
between work in the physical sciences and work in the
humanities and the social sciences is not at all exclusively
in method. The disparity has to do with the application
of the same method to different kinds of materials. In
the social sciences and the humanities the data, that is,
the facts involved, are not always reducible to the physical
and frequently do not lend themselves to quantification.
It would be much more constructive if social scientists and
humanists consistently emphasized their difference from
the physical scientists in terms of the materials studied and
then by means of rigorous scientific method proceeded to
clarify and to explain the precise nature of this difference
and the importance of the recognition of the difference for
society and culture in general.

The only sustained argument of this thesis that I know
of in English was done recently by an American scholar
of Polish origin and training. I refer, of course, to the
book of Professor Florian Znaniecki which bears the
title, *Cultural Sciences, Their Origin and Development*
(Urbana, 1952).[21]

Contrary, then, to the American bias that everything
that smacks of the " mentalistic " is unworthy and even
incapable of serious, rational examination, I repeat that
I regard all cultural phenomena (and by this I do not
refer exclusively to the culture of primitive peoples in
the anthropological sense) as capable of scientific study,
and that I believe that American scholarship must mature
rapidly to the point where it recognizes this as an absolute

necessity and then sets about translating the notion into action. In brief, I am of the firm opinion that we can no longer afford to regard the humanities and the theoretical aspects of the social sciences as the mayonnaise on the bourgeois salad. Time is running out, and we need a most rigorously intellectual re-examination of the premises on which our culture is based. Otherwise the cultivation of our culture will die of neglect.

The history of the term *cultural sciences*, which as yet sounds strange to most American ears, is an intriguing one, but time necessitates postponing a fuller discussion of it till another occasion. It should, however, be briefly remarked in passing that the term *cultural science* comes to us via German translations of the dichotomy originally established in John Locke's essay, the dichotomy of physical science as opposed to moral science.

In 1849 a German translation of John Stuart Mill's *Logic* by one I. Schiel for the first time, probably, consistently used the term *Geisteswissenschaften* for "moral science," beginning with the sixth book of Mill's second volume, which bears the title "On the Logic of the Moral Sciences." The term *Geisteswissenschaften* attains to a classical usage in Germany at the hands of Wilhelm Dilthey with the publication in 1883 of his justly famous *Introduction to the Cultural Sciences* (*Einleitung in die Geisteswissenschaften*).

In the 1890's in Germany, however, there was a concerted effort by such scholars as Windelband, Rickert and Weber to substitute for *Geisteswissenschaften* the terms *Geschichtswissenschaft* (historical science) and *Kulturwissenschaft* (cultural science). The desire to substitute these two terms arose from the wish to emphasize method rather than content. The historical sciences dealt, so it was pointed out, with concrete specifics as opposed to theoretical abstractions.

Stemming from Alexander Pope's famous dictum and August Comte's *études de l'humanité*, it has recently been suggested that these sciences might better be called the sciences of man because they aspire to the Greek ideal of know thyself and are concerned with the study of man's constitution or reconstitution of the universe. Significantly, then, Professor H. A. Hodges, a British scholar, in a recent book on Wilhelm Dilthey suggests and argues for the term the *human studies* as an adequate and possibly as the best translation for the German term *Geisteswissenschaft*.[22] It now remains to be seen how successful Florian Znaniecki's book will be in helping to establish the term *cultural sciences*.

I am not merely suggesting the adoption of a new term for its own sake. If the term *cultural sciences* or, for that matter, *human studies* or the *sciences of man*, acquires general usage, I want that term to connote two things. One of them is the assumption that all cultural phenomena can and should be studied with scientific rigor. The other connotation for which I fervently hope is that of systematically developed scientific teamwork among the humanists on the one hand, among the social scientists on the other hand, and ultimately between these two groups. I alluded earlier to the 1952 Indiana Conference of Anthropologists and Linguists,[23] the 1951 Cornell Conference of Linguists and Psychologists and the Indiana Summer Seminar on Psycholinguistics of 1953.[24] The 1953 Chicago Conference on Ethnolinguistics,[25] and the 1953 MLA Interdisciplinary Seminar on Language and Culture [26] are additional illustrations of this kind of interdisciplinary scientific teamwork.

119

Actually, however, conferences are too occasional and sporadic, as are seminars established by learned societies. Siegfried Giedion, the distinguished author of *Space-Time and Architecture* (Cambridge, 1941) and of *Mechanization Takes Command* (New York, 1948), and significantly an art historian by profession but an engineer and architect by training, spoke on our campus some dozen odd years ago about the necessity for universities to establish and maintain what he called super-faculties. He meant by this simply teams of scholars representing allied disciplines who would be assigned the task of and allowed the time for the systematic study of the structures of the major areas of learning. So, for example, a team comprising a literary scholar, a linguist, an art historian, a musicologist, and an esthetician would attempt systematic work in correlating the scholarship of these related disciplines, particularly from the point of view of establishing common research goals and common methods for achieving them. Similar kinds of teams would attack the common problems of the physical and biological and social sciences. As you know, the crisis of the last World War made such teamwork in the physical sciences mandatory and thus produced the Great Bomb. One of the immediate products of such team research would be the important awareness of a diversity of what the late Professor Hans Leisegang calls *Denkformen* (Berlin, 1952), that is, the varying logical structures that underlie the various disciplines. A physicist, for example, does not think of his discipline and does not attack its problems in the same way as does, let us say, a sociologist or an art historian. Each of these scholars operates with a different set of assumptions, although all of them seek Joseph Conrad's common goal of truth. The quest for truth will obviously be rewarded in greater measure to the extent that common-alities and differences between the disciplines are clarified.

Only the universities, unless it be the state, can provide the facilities for this kind of teamwork. But the eminent biologist, Ludwig von Bartalanffy of the University of Ottawa, only recently complained in *The Scientific Monthly* (November, 1953) that he has failed to persuade any Canadian or American university to initiate team studies of what he has been calling General System Theory. General System Theory involves precisely the problem of the diversity of underlying logic and method in the various sciences.

In the cultural sciences, I regret to say, the advocates of the kind of scholarly teamwork that I have been discuss-ing are principally European. The Americans of this persuasion are almost exclusively of European origin or training, as, for example, Florian Znaniecki.

In brief summary, I have been trying to say that if religion is one of the great motivating forces of human thought and action, and I think there can be no doubt that it is, then religion and its manifestations should be rigorously studied. I have argued further that I believe that all cultural phenomena, including, of course, religion, can be studied scientifically as are the material aspects of the universe. I have implied that an adequate scientific study of religion requires the combined and sustained efforts of all of the disciplines devoted to the study of man, that is, the cultural sciences. Finally, I have maintained that American universities particularly have been remiss in providing the opportunity and the facility for organized team research, especially in the cultural sciences and with particular reference to religious phenomena. Following Mr. Kennan, I suggest that this deplorable condition may be owing to fundamental weaknesses in the American national character. (See Introduction, p. 5 f.) If that be so, then it behooves the American public to direct its universities to do something about the matter. In addition to a radical change of heart on the part of substantial numbers of the faculty, this would also require substantial financial support. I continue to believe, however, and so do you, I am sure, that the scientific re-examination and validation of the bases of American culture were never more urgent or worthwhile.

References

INTRODUCTION

¹ See Philips P. Moulton, "Is Religion Too Controversial?" *AAUP Bulletin*, XXXIX (1953), 398-403.

² *New York Herald Tribune*, May 20, 1953. For more of the same see Lewis Mumford, "The Napoleon of Notting Hill," *New Republic*, November 18, 1954, regarding Arnold Toynbee.

³ *New Republic*, March 29, 1954, p. 19 f.; quoted with the permission of the *New Republic*.

⁴ *New Republic*, March 1, 1954, p. 20.

⁵ Cited by Thomas Mann in "Freud's Position in the History of Modern Thought," in *Past Masters* (New York, 1933), pp. 169-170.

⁶ See Franz Alexander, *Our Age of Unreason* (New York, 1942).

⁷ Eugene Exman, "Reading, Writing, and Religion," *Harper's Magazine*, CCVI (May, 1953), 84.

⁸ Erich Fromm, *Man for Himself* (New York, 1947).

⁹ Compare Peter Viereck, Section 9, "What Kind of Conservatism?" of *Shame and Glory of the Intellectuals* (Boston, 1953), p. 266: "Facism is not capitalism or any other economics, but a state of mind. It is a surrender of the soul to evil, to the temptation of power, to the particularly murderous brand of evil that results when you substitute egotistic domineering for Christian self-restraint and when you substitute hate for mutual sympathy and substitute pre-Christian, tribal loyalties of blood for post-Christian brotherhood."—Quoted with the kind permission of Beacon Press, Inc., the publishers.

CHAPTER ONE

¹ Joseph Wood Krutch, *The Modern Temper* (New York, 1929), pp. 14 and 16; quoted with the permission of the author and the publishers, Harcourt, Brace and Co.

² *Bulletin of the Atomic Scientists*, IV (October, 1948), 300 ff.

³ *The New Yorker*, March 3, 1951, p. 21.

⁴ René Descartes, "Discourse on Method," *The Philosophical Works of Descartes*, Vol. I, tr. by Haldane and Ross (Cambridge,

REFERENCES

1911), p. 119; quoted with the permission of the publishers, Cambridge University Press.

[5] Galileo, "Letter to Grand Duchess Christine," quoted by J. H. Randall, Jr. in *The Making of the Modern Mind* (New York, 1926), p. 239.

[6] Arthur Miller, *Death of a Salesman* (New York, 1949), pp. 82 and 138.

[7] John Locke, *Selections*, ed. by S. P. Pamprecht (New York, 1928), p. 111.

[8] William James, "The Will to Believe," in *Basic Problems of Philosophy: Selected Readings*, by Bronstein, Krikorian, and Wiener (New York, 1947), p. 545.

[9] Albert Schweitzer, *The Quest of the Historical Jesus*, tr. by W. Montgomery (New York, 1948), p, 403; quoted with the permission of the publishers, The Macmillan Company.

CHAPTER THREE

[1] A. J. Heschel, *Man Is Not Alone* (New York, 1951), p. 55.

[2] The verb *tacam* always means to perceive, to taste. The noun is also used in the sense of judgment. In our passage Targum renders the word *ta amu* with " realize "; the Septuagint, *geisasthe* with " taste." Compare Seforno's commentary *ad locum*, " taste, namely feel with your sense and *see* with the eye of reason that God is good."

[3] Compare the references in Brown-Driver-Briggs, *A Hebrew and English Lexicon of the Old Testament* (Oxford, 1906), p. 761.

[4] *Collected Papers of Charles S. Peirce*, edited by Charles Hartshorn and Paul Weiss (Cambridge, 1934), V, 45; quoted with the permission of Harvard University Press, the publishers.

[5] *Theaetetus*, 155d.

[6] *Metaphysics*, Is, 182b12.

[7] *Mechanics*, 847a11.

[8] " The facts of the case from first to last are so wonderful that we venture to say that no general impression of Nature reached along scientific or any other lines can be even in the direction of being true that does not sound the note of joyous appreciation and of reverent wonder."—J. A. Thompson at the end of his Gifford Lectures on *The System of Animate Nature* (New York, 1920), p. 650; quoted with the permission of Henry Holt and Company, Inc., the publishers.

[9] *The Works of Francis Thompson*, III, 80-81.

[10] William Blake, *A Vision of the Last Judgment*.

[11] A. J. Heschel, *op. cit.*, pp. 11 ff.

[12] *Ibid.*, p. 76.

[13] *Nabhal.* See Brown-Driver-Briggs, *op. cit.*, p. 614.

[14] A. J. Heschel, *op. cit.*, p. 68.

[15] For a more extended analysis of the ideas of this lecture, see A. J. Heschel, *God in Search of Man. A Philosophy of Judaism*, published in December, 1955.

CHAPTER FIVE

[1] Henry Alden Bunker, "Psychoanalysis and the Study of Religion," *Psychoanalysis and the Social Sciences* (New York, 1951), III, 7-34.

[2] Edward Hitschmann, "New Varieties of Religious Experience," *Psychoanalysis and the Social Sciences*, I (1947), 195-233.

[3] Friedrich Nietzsche, letter to his sister, 11 June 1865.

[4] Quoted from Bunker, *op. cit.*, pp. 7-9, with the permission of the publishers, International Universities Press, Inc.

[5] Sigmund Freud, "The Antithetical Sense of Primal Words," *Collected Papers*, IV, 184.

[6] Quoted by Hitschmann, *op. cit.*, p. 199; reprinted with the permission of the publishers, International Universities Press, Inc.

[7] See in this connection also, for example, P. Zacharias, "*Die Bedeutung der Psychologie C. G. Jungs für die christliche Theologie,*" *Zeitschrift für Religions- und Geistesgeschichte*, V (1953), 257-269.

[8] The quotations from Freud's essay are given in part by Bunker, p. 10.

[9] Hitschmann, *op. cit.*, p. 196; quoted with the permission of the publishers, International Universities Press, Inc.

[10] *New York Times*, February 21, 1954.

[11] Quoted by Hitschmann, *op. cit.*, p. 199; reprinted with the permission of the publishers, International Universities Press, Inc.

[12] From "The Psychoanalytic Study of Religion," *Journal of Abnormal and Social Psychology*, XXXIII (1938), 450; see also Karl Stern's *The Third Revolution: A Study of Psychiatry and Religion* (New York, 1954), which appeared shortly after this lecture was given and hence too late for inclusive treatment.

[13] See Clyde Kluckhohn, "Universal Categories of Culture," in *Anthropology Today*, ed. by A. Kroeber (Chicago, 1953), p. 507.

[14] In this connection I should like to cite what I regard as the most under-rated book of the decade, *viz.*, Roderick Seidenberg, *Posthistoric Man: An Inquiry* (Chapel Hill, 1950).

[15] *New Republic*, February 15, 1954. Reprinted with the permission of the *New Republic*.

[16] Karl Marx, *A Contribution to the Critique of Political Economy*, tr. by M. I. Stone (New York, 1904), pp. 11-12.

[17] John C. Murray, "The Natural Law," in *Great Expressions of Human Rights*, ed. by R. N. MacIver (New York, 1950), pp. 88-91, 95. The italics are mine.—H. A. B. Reprinted with the permission of the Institute for Religious and Social Studies, holder of the copyright.

[18] *New Republic*, July 13, 1953. Reprinted with the permission of the *New Republic*.

[19] See Harold Taylor, "The Philosophical Foundations of General Education," in *The Fifty-First Year Book of the National Society for the Study of Education*, ed. by Nelson B. Henry, Part I, General Education (Chicago, 1952), pp. 20-45.

[20] George Sarton, *The Life of Science* (New York, 1948), p. 177.

[21] See also John Higham, "Intellectual History and Its Neighbors," *Journal of the History of Ideas*, XV (1954), 344-6 for a discussion of the essential differences between the social sciences and the humanities.

[22] H. A. Hodges, *Wilhelm Dilthey, An Introduction* (New York, 1944); also *The Philosophy of Wilhelm Dilthey* (London, 1952).

For further documentation and discussion of the history of the terms see Erich Rothacker, *Logik und Systematik der Geisteswissenschaften* (Bonn, 1947), Florian Znaniecki, *Cultural Sciences* (Urbana, 1952), Ernst Cassirer, *Zur Logik der Kulturwissenschaften* (Göteborg, 1942), and *The Problem of Knowledge* (New Haven, 1950). In the latter, Charles W. Hendel's note 2 in the Preface, p. 3, is relevant; also Carl Brinkmann's article "Geisteswissenschaften" in the *Encyclopedia of the Social Sciences*, ed. E. R. A. Seligman (New York, 1935), vol. VI.

[23] See *Results of the Conferences of Anthropologists and Linguists*, *International Journal of American Linguistics*, Memoir 8 (Baltimore, 1953).

[24] John B. Carroll *et al.*, *Report and Recommendations of the Interdisciplinary Summer Seminar in Psychology and Linguistics* (Ithaca, 1951), mimeograph; Charles E. Osgood, Thomas Sebeok, *et al.*, *Psycholinguistics, A Survey of Theory and Research Problems*, Memoir 10 of the *International Journal of American Linguistics* (Baltimore, 1954).

[25] See Harry Hoijer, ed., *Language in Culture: Conference on the Interrelations of Language and Other Aspects of Culture* (also published as Memoir 79 of the American Anthropological Association) (Chicago, 1954).

[26] "Developing Cultural Understanding Through Foreign Language Study: A Report of the MLA Interdisciplinary Seminar in Language and Culture," *PMLA*, LXVIII (1953), 1196-1218.

Biographical Notes

BASILIUS, HAROLD A. Professor of German and Director of the Humanities Program at Wayne University, Detroit. A graduate of Concordia Seminary and Ohio State University (Ph. D., 1935), Dr. Basilius began his teaching career in 1929 as an instructor of German at Capital University in Columbus, Ohio. He came to Wayne in 1936 as Professor and Head of the Department of German, after five years on the faculty of the University of Chicago. In addition to numerous articles in professional journals, Dr. Basilius is the author of *A Workbook for Reading German*, published by the Wayne University Press in 1939.

BERTHOLD, FRED, JR. Chairman of the Department of Religion, Dartmouth College, Hanover, New Hampshire. A graduate of Dartmouth in 1945, he received the Bachelor of Divinity degree in 1947 from the University of Chicago. The year following he took further graduate work at Columbia University and during 1948-49 taught philosophy in Utica, New York. Professor Berthold was ordained a minister in the Plymouth Congregational Church in Utica in 1949. He has been a member of the Dartmouth faculty since 1949 and became Assistant Professor of Religion in 1951. He is the author of several articles on subjects dealing with religion and psychology and was a Fellow on the Blatchford Foundation at the Chicago Theological Seminary, University of Chicago, from which he received the Ph. D. degree in 1954.

DAVIES, A. POWELL. Minister, All Souls Unitarian Church, Washington, D. C. Born in Birkenhead, England, Dr. Davies received his B. D. from Richmond College, University of

127

London, in 1925, and his D. D. from Meadville in 1947. He came to the United States with his wife and two children in 1928. A Methodist minister between 1925-33, Dr. Davies has been a Unitarian since 1933. He has been pastor at All Souls since 1944. As an author, Dr. Davies has contributed to magazines and written four books. His latest is *The Urge to Persecute*, 1954.

HESCHEL, ABRAHAM JOSHUA. Associate Professor of Jewish Ethics and Mysticism at the Jewish Theological Seminary of America, New York City, since 1944. Dr. Heschel earned his Ph. D. at the University of Berlin in 1932. He has served on the staffs of the Institute for Jewish Studies (Berlin), the University of Warsaw, and the Hebrew Union College in Cincinnati, Ohio. Dr. Heschel was formerly a director of Jewish Adult Education in Frankfurt, Germany. He is the author of numerous articles and books of which a recent one is *Man's Quest for God*, 1954.

TILLICH, PAUL. Formerly Professor of Theology at Union Theological Seminary, New York City, now Professor of Religion at Harvard University. Born in Starzeddel, Kreis Guben, Prussia, Dr. Tillich studied at several European institutions including the Universities of Berlin, Tübingen and Halle. He received a Ph. D. degree from the University of Breslau in 1911. Before coming to the United States in 1933, Dr. Tillich held teaching positions at a number of well-known German universities. He was privatdozent of theology at the University of Berlin, 1919-24, professor of theology at the University of Marburg, 1924-24, University of Dresden, 1925-29, University of Leipzig, 1928-29, and professor of philosophy at the University of Frankfort-am-Main, 1929-33. He is author of *The Religious Situation, The Interpretation of History, The Protestant Era*, and a number of other books and periodical articles.